The Consistent Choice

Also by Donna Kendall

Sailing on an Ocean of Tears

Dancing with Bianchina

Stitch-a-Story

Uncle Charlie's Soup

The Consistent Choice

For Better Living in a Better World

Donna Kendall

ISBN: 978-1-4525-6014-4 (sc)
ISBN: 978-1-4525-6015-1 (hc)
ISBN: 978-1-4525-6013-7 (e)

Library of Congress Control Number: 2012918661

Balboa Press books may be ordered through booksellers or by contacting:

Balboa Press
A Division of Hay House
1663 Liberty Drive
Bloomington, IN 47403
www.balboapress.com
1-(877) 407-4847

Printed in the United States of America

Balboa Press rev. date: 11/1/2012

For My Parents

Angelo and Giulia,

Who taught me all about love and choices…

Table of Contents

Preface

Former Secretary of State, Henry Kissinger, once stated that "The ordinary event can be dealt with by routine – a procedure established in advance of a given eventuality." The average person is confronted with many ordinary events throughout the course of a day that may require some type of action, decision, or attention. The wisdom of finding a central routine that can help one manage all the possible "eventualities" which challenge our daily lives can have a positive impact on the short term and long term decisions we make. Each day we find that we base many decisions on established routines, the consequences of which shape the course of life for its duration.

Consider the factors involved in the purchase of an automobile. Style, efficiency, mileage, needs, status, performance, and so on, all play a part in the choice of a vehicle whose main function is to transport us to our destinations. The decision to operate a certain type of vehicle can rely on habit – such as, we've always purchased a Chevy, or upon a diligent attempt to purchase the right vehicle to meet our current needs. Consequently, many judgments can be made about a person by observing the kind of vehicle they drive. A Mitsubishi Lancer or Nissan Maxima says something uniquely different about the owner as compared with the driver of a Ford Focus or Fiesta. From the simplest decision to the most complex we are evaluated by the consequences of our decisions. Our everyday decisions say something about us, whether exercised routinely or after considerable thought and planning. Choice of vehicles is just one way to surmise the interests, inclinations and values of someone unknown. The car a person drives, the clothes they wear, the homes in which they choose to live, as well as the devices they use to communicate with others become a visible résumé for what they value, but it may be misinterpreted by many, and judgments passed may be inaccurate. A person is more than the things they own. What a person values is dependent on what they *do* with those things. And what they do comes back to the routines they have established.

Needs change throughout the course of a lifetime which ultimately affect the decisions we make and how those decisions are executed. On occasion, we may be held accountable and challenged to explain, defend, or justify our decisions. If the decision being questioned is the result of routine and made without much thought, one can shrug their shoulders and respond with *I've always done it this way.* However, if some degree of deliberation or reflection was involved in the choice, a thoughtful response may be necessary. If we have nothing else in this world, we have two things: life and choice. How intricately woven these two endowments truly are merits careful scrutiny. Without life, we have no choice; without choice we have an existence, but not a full life. Modern idioms about life have taken the place of philosophical examination. *I have a new lease on life; It's my life; Get a life; As large as life*, and so on… are expressions that try to send an indistinct message about life but when we stack these expressions up against the more serious, underlying messages, it can be a more daunting experience. This book is meant to be an invitation to consider life more carefully and to embrace a lifestyle that chooses loving options directed toward life-affirming actions. Life demands that we learn from our past choices and continually renew an effort to choose the options that provide us with the authentic freedom that we are meant to enjoy.

Why Examine Choice?

Human development and learning has resulted from a steady stream of choices, decisions and consequences. From the time one reaches an age when there is some control over decision-making, life is filled with an array of good and evil intentions, right and wrong options, and positive and negative outcomes. As children, our choices may not be calculated or well-considered; a toddler's choices are often governed by stretching the free-will muscles to see how they work. However, once a child's cognitive development increases, so does the sophistication of their choices. Children begin to rely less on impulse and innate behaviors, and discover that certain outcomes result from poor choices. As we grow and become more comfortable with this process we begin to see choices for what they are: opportunities for potential growth, stagnation, or harm. The complexity of human decision-making is a quality that separates us from other living species. Animals do not see the end of their existence as a possible outcome of their decisions. People, as more advanced creatures, are able to contemplate ourselves, our actions, our future – not solely as individuals but as a family of persons. As the human race has worked to become more civilized, it is important to remember that growth is the result of human choices. We continue to grow as we learn from our choices – from error as well as success. Yet, not unlike mice in a maze, from the very first choice made by humanity to the complexity of choices we face today, we struggle for the outcome that provides us with a reward, or, possibly more choices.

The worst possible fate is a dead-end choice. The best case scenario is the alternative that provides us with additional opportunities that foster a pattern of growth by doing the least amount of harm.

As recorded in the Old Testament, humanity began its very existence with a life-altering choice, and from the very beginning God has honored our choices above everything else, for one of the greatest gifts we have received as living beings is *free will*. God created us with an aptitude for decision-making. We might well have been created otherwise, but the fact that we may choose to exercise this will for what is good or what is not good for us, is evidence that *choices* are woven into the very fabric of our being. From the Judeo-Christian account of the creation of Adam and Eve, one of the first things to confront this newly created couple was a set of instructions, followed by a choice. In the book of Genesis, God had commanded "You are free to eat from any tree in the garden; but you must not eat from the tree of knowledge of good and evil, for when you eat of it you will surely die" (Gn. 2:16-17). God had presented humanity with a choice from the very beginning, and from that first moment, *Choose Life* was a difficult choice to make.

As the first recorded decision ever made by human beings appeared to have been a life and death decision, it subsequently demonstrates the significance of every human decision since then. Why give humans such a definitive choice? Did they understand that it was a critical life-and-death choice? They were told it was, and yet they chose an option that perhaps *seemed right at the time*. If one supposes that this first recorded decision was the prototype for all succeeding decisions and that every decision is in some respect a life-or-death choice, it encourages us to examine all our decisions more carefully. Presumably, each day is another chance to remake that first decision made by the human race that chose some kind of harm over good. With each new day humanity plays out that scene again and again – the opportunity to make a choice that is life-giving over one that serves a different purpose.

The value of understanding the relationship between choice and desired outcome often comes down to motive. There is an innate need to serve a known, or even an unknown purpose with each decision that is made, but the old adage, "you can't always have your cake and eat it too" comes back to haunt us. We wish to have positive outcomes for both positive and negative choices. Professor Gregory Foster in his article "Ethics: Time to Revisit the Basics" explains,

> "When we seek to determine the rightness or wrongness of something, we should do so with two major criteria in mind: truth and justice. Ralph Waldo Emerson made the monumentally insightful observation that 'truth is the summit of being; justice is the application of it [truth] to affairs.' The two go hand in hand. Ethics—ethical reasoning, ethical choice, ethical conduct—requires that we seek the truth, the pinnacle of life, in order to have a proper basis—the only legitimate basis—for achieving justice. Justice served is ethics realized" (The Humanist).

By making consistent ethical choices, and choosing the life-result over the destructive choice, it is necessary to factor in truth and justice for the benefit of life, so that our choices rely on a beneficial and natural routine. Dr. Foster goes on to remind us that

> "Habit is programmed repetition, the routinization of thought by which we remove presumably mundane matters to our subconscious so they can be dealt with more efficiently or conveniently without the attendant need to constantly revisit first principles."

In order to make consistent life-affirming choices, one must align all thoughts within the parameters of truth that is motivated by justice. This alignment is often challenged by the needs of the moment, to which little thought about truth and justice may be given.

Quite often, the bombardment of choices with which we are confronted on a daily basis can be overwhelming. It takes a concerted effort to entrust our intellect with the duty of making the decision to choose life among all our options. Most often, small decisions don't appear to be life-or-death. It often appears that larger decisions are more crucial – we *know* when those decisions come along and they can be agonizing. Yet, because habitual decisions are often at the mercy of non-thinking processes, it becomes even more critical to adjust all thoughts toward the ultimate good by making life-giving, moral and ethical choices. To illustrate this point, consider the cereal aisle of any grocery store in the United States and suddenly everything we understand about life and choices comes into sharper focus. Where did all these choices come from? Not only are there choices of cereal brands, but choices within those brands with regard to types of grains, flavors, shapes, flakes, clusters, charms, fruits, crunchiness, nutritive value, and so on. The cereal aisle may well be a microcosm of the world in which we live and a fair evaluation of our decision-making capabilities. Do we have the time to investigate which cereal is right for us? Are we so overwhelmed with choices that we pick up what we've always eaten, or do we feel adventurous and try something new? Have our choices been influenced by an advertisement? Or have we perhaps stopped caring and decide on whatever looks good that day, or something that's on sale? While grocery shopping may not necessarily seem to involve ethical or moral decision-making, it can be a daunting exercise in life skills, and the cereal aisle is only one path in the montage of consumer decisions. In the big scheme of things, the cereal aisle may seem like a pretty safe place where the choices confronting us may not seem life-threatening.

However, a choice as apparently simple as which cereal to eat can have potential consequences beyond our understanding. If the upshot of our cereal preference affected our taste buds alone, we might perhaps choose something incredibly sweet, with ample additives that enhance the flavor. As we know, our taste buds are not the only body part affected by our food preferences. Other cells in the human body are affected by high levels of sugar and additives. Still, if our sweeter selections affected our personal health alone, unhealthy choices might well be excused, but as genetics and biology confirm, once we reproduce, our children may carry the DNA that predisposes them to diseases complicated by eating too much sugar.

If one's decisions affected no one else than the individual then what difference would it make what choices were made; choice would carry little, or no burden. If, however, one stops to consider how each choice affects an entire race of human beings, then it seems prudent that our choices should be more carefully evaluated. The reality is that each individual decision does not affect the decision-maker alone. Humans are all connected: genetically, socially, spiritually, economically, politically, and scientifically. We do not live in isolated bubbles – we are all an integral part of a created world. Regardless of one's beliefs or understanding of how creation came to be, the fact remains: humanity is not composed of isolated beings disconnected from one another. We are united by DNA, and we all share the same home – the planet Earth. Through our choices we have the power to create the kind of world in which we'd prefer to live – we remake these choices each and every day. As individual humans, and as collective humanity, we are the sum of our choices. If we can refocus our intentions and grow into a habit of choosing life in both the mundane and seemingly insignificant decisions, as well as those more critical, then perhaps we can evolve into a human race that perseveres for the good of all. A human person is the most precious thing there is, and as humans we want solid affirmation about every choice we make. The goal is to take a closer look at how our liberties and freedoms combined with our rights to choose have sometimes put us at odds with ourselves. Putting all our choices on the same page may affect a desired outcome shared by all.

Life thoughts

Individual growth is governed by individual choices but can still be profoundly affected by the choices of others. It's a reciprocal affectation; our choices affect others and their choices affect us. In order for true growth to occur in humanity, our individual and collective choices must be integrated. For the strongest principle of growth to benefit everyone, the human choice must be geared toward advancing all of humanity.

From Origins to Destinations

"Life and death have long played a central role in anthropology's efforts to define the human. Recent developments in the experience of both, however, suggest reconfigurations in these essential thresholds of being and a corresponding need to reexamine the analytic assumptions brought to bear on them. Alongside the emergence of new forms of biological science, medical technology and expertise, a concern for life pervades both international political discourse and the rhetoric of international moralism. Both individual bodies and figures of mass death feature prominently in political stagecraft, while calculations of risk define and measure life conditions. In addition to recognizing the emergence of humanitarianism, human rights, and ecology as key secular domains central to the construction of valued life, we ask participants to rethink classic topics in politics, ethics, kinship and religion around this concern for being and nonbeing. What phenomena mark an era that rediscovers economy in terms of precariousness, and sanctions state torture in the name of security? What new ghosts might it produce? How have these changes unsettled kinship, generations, and human horizons of the future by reconfiguring relations between the living and the dead or the young and the old?" (The Society for Cultural Anthropology: Life and Death, A Conversation, Spring SCA meeting).

Cultural anthropology is a science dedicated to understanding our humanness in all the contexts of daily life including, but not limited to, how we perceive the world around us through art, literature, music and religion; how we structure our governments, hierarchies, families, and social and economic paradigms; as well as our behaviors, traditions and customs. The sum of who we have become as a species is the result of millions of years of decisions, both individual and collective. From the very beginning our innate nature fostered a need to balance our individual needs against those of the collective.

Early humans were tribal. Survival of the species depended upon the ability to defend ourselves against predators or other tribes. We needed to rely on communal strength to help us in situations where as individuals we could not face the danger alone. A struggle between satisfying the individual versus meeting the needs of the group developed and has plagued the human race since the very beginning. What causes harm to the community may cause harm to the individual, and what causes harm to the individual may cause harm to the community. Similarly, what benefits one person may benefit the group, and what benefits the group may benefit the person. The burning question remains: how can we make choices that benefit both the individual and the collective when the ultimate goal of life on the planet is to maintain and improve life?

Newborn babies illustrate our most primitive instincts, those behaviors which require no decision-making as a result of learning through experience. Newborns begin to breathe air, to sleep, to eat, to cry, and to seek comfort from others, primarily the mother, without how-to lessons. As babies grow and develop they begin to rely less on instincts and more on learned behavior – this affects cognitive, physical, emotional, intellectual and social development. Over time we develop self-control and self-discipline to outgrow limited instinctual behavior. Without this type of growth and development, we would always succumb to our momentary needs and instinctual behaviors whenever the mood hits us. Curling up in a ball and going to sleep at work when we feel tired would result in written reprimands and possibly job loss. How well-disciplined we are becomes the value by which we measure our development as a human being. "The more disciplined behavior (behavior determined by intellect) displayed by the individual, the more human he becomes. The less disciplined behavior (behavior in response to instinct) displayed by the individual, the more he becomes like the lower order of animals that are lacking in intellect and are driven by their instincts" (onelife.com).

To achieve the highest level of our humanness requires that we advance beyond our neonatal instincts and progress toward self-actualization, but this involves regulating behavior away from impulse and more toward reasoned decisions because the goal of self-discipline is to be responsible citizens. If we each lived completely alone on an island, there would be no need for self-discipline; we could eat and sleep when we please, behave in any manner that satisfied the needs of the moment and there would be no need for rules governing self-restraint since our own behaviors would affect no one else but ourselves. If we wish to live our lives with the intent of satisfying the individual but cannot acknowledge that our actions will have an effect on others, then we are up against an unrealistic fantasy. Our choices must take into consideration the effect we will have on others. With each decision we make that affects the self, we affect the whole. There is not one single decision we can make that does not have a ripple effect. It may not be immediately obvious, sometimes it takes many years to see the result, but the course of human history reveals that whatever plagued us on *Day One* of our existence continues to plague us today.

The Old Testament is filled with stories that reflect the beliefs, traditions, and spiritual growth of the human race that began with an impressive account of creation, where God as the Creator of all things, looked upon his creation and deemed that it was good. Within a few short pages we encounter the most defining moment in all of human history. In the book of Genesis we read the story of our human infancy where God created human beings and placed them in a wonderful place and surrounded them with the beauty and goodness of his creation. Among the most beautiful gifts on the earth was the essence and wonder of variety. If everything had been completely the same in the world; if there were only one thing to eat, only one kind of plant or animal, only one color, only one type of person, etc…, there would be no need for decisions or choices. But the world has an abundance of goods, and along with those goods, we have the freedom to choose. Dilemma was the result of choice. Whether we consider the first decision-making humans, or our own personal decision-making development, choice is the very first thing that happens to us as human beings once our instinctual behavior confronts our intellect and conscience. We are responsible for making numerous choices. The decisions of early human beings have somehow affected life as we know it today. If we have learned nothing else we should recognize that an individual's choices do not impact the individual alone, but make an impression on each member of our world, because we are not disconnected from one another, not by time, space, or actions.

In everything there is a choice and with each choice we have free will, and with this freedom there is responsibility. With responsibility comes the broader understanding that we are part of a large human family and we owe humanity our best decisions. Around the year 1910, *The London Times* posed a question as an invitation for essays to write on the theme: "What is wrong with the world?" In response to this question, G.K. Chesterton, writer, philosopher, and journalist, replied with the following letter:

> Dear Sirs:
> I am.
> Sincerely yours,
> G. K. Chesterton

What plagues humanity as a whole begins with the individual. As a human being *I* am the sum of the choices I've made. As a culture of people *we* are the sum of billions of individual choices. We are all connected to one another, and sometimes we choose to remember that, and at other times, if it proves to be inconvenient, we choose to forget. If a person understood how even a simple choice could affect the human race, would choices be evaluated more carefully? We do not live in solitary worlds of our own making – we are part of an interconnected world. There is a *physical* thread that connects us to every other human being and to other living things, but there is also the thread of caring and concern that connects us as well. Humans have always shared this planet as our home and through the gift of choice we have had the power to create the kind of world in which we'd like to live.

From an historical perspective, human decisions and the effects of those decisions on the course of human existence, is best understood when see ourselves as the unwitting beneficiaries of the choices made by our ancestors, and as the authors of our descendants' problems. Generally speaking, people are still tribal, as seen in social groupings, cliques, and the lines of political divisions and the sub-factions that share common agendas. The problem is that even within the tribes there is dissention and contradictions when it comes to making choices. In recent events, divisions arose with regard to poor decisions made by corporate overindulgence. Most people agreed enough was enough – however, did all the members of Occupy Wall Street stop eating at McDonalds, give up their iphones, stop purchasing products such as GM vehicles, flat-screen televisions, and state-of-the-art technology as a statement against corporate greed? How is individual greed reflected back on to the protesters? It is time to consider the inheritance and endowment factor that continues the chain of our human weaknesses. Have we inherited envy and therefore, now possess greed, and which of these traits will we bequeath unto the next generation? Must future generations be plagued with the duty of unraveling the mixed messages they witness on every level of morality based on our current decisions?

In the April, 1998 UNESCO article entitled, "The Ethics of the Future," Federico Mayor Zaragoza wrote,

> "All over the world, the citizens of today are claiming rights over the citizens of tomorrow, threatening their well-being and at times their lives. I repeat: today's citizens are claiming rights over tomorrow's, and we are beginning to realize that we are jeopardizing the exercise by future generations of their human rights."

The choices our citizens make today will affect the human rights of tomorrow's citizens – of this there is no doubt. By making choices that promote life and open new decision-making opportunities for the future we may guide our human race back to the recognition of its dignity and consequently bequeath to our children a culture of peace that is accomplished by acknowledging human rights and human life. We must relearn to love in the broader sense of the word – not only ourselves as individuals with rights but as vital members of the entire human race.

In one of his most fundamental teaching principles found in the New Testament, Jesus of Nazareth gave the command "Love your neighbor as yourself," (Mk 12:31) and in doing so he transcended our understanding of human responsibility. In the course of making a decision that is good for the self, there is the understanding that it must be good for all, today and tomorrow.

Good decision-making does not always take into account the good of all, or even love for that matter. There are times when decision-making is based on sensory stimuli, intuition, emotion-based reasoning, or analytical deliberate reasoning. In addition to decisions made by experience, there are often those made by emotional responses or calculated objectives. It is with the recognition of alternatives that decision-making advances beyond a mere *reaction*. When all our alternatives are derived from desired life-giving outcomes humans may progress above satisfying primal needs and a greater purpose may be achieved. As Helen Keller once said, "Until the great mass of the people shall be filled with the sense of responsibility for each other's welfare, social justice can never be attained."

Life thoughts

Human DNA is composed of millions of past choices made by our ancestors – their habits, with whom they bore children, their lifestyles, and acquired dependencies. Our present DNA is affected by our current choices and these choices will become the building blocks of our descendants' traits.

Human morality is as ingrained in us as the physical DNA which we can now see. It has taken its "cues" from the past, from the triumphs and mistakes made by those who came before us. Our present morality is a reflection of cultural revolutions and attitudes, both past and present. In order to lay a more solid foundation for future generations, we must be more unified when considering what that foundation will look like.

The Finite Choice

Bumper stickers and some T-shirts are fascinating tools with which we may become even remotely familiar with strangers we encounter. We can learn a lot about the person behind the wheel by reading their bumper stickers, or by reading some fascinating logo on their clothing. Some slogans are evidence of a person's sense of humor:

> "Cleanliness is a sign of a sick mind."
>
> "The last person to follow me this closely bought this bumper."
>
> "Very funny, Scotty; now beam down my clothes."

While other slogans suggest more serious concerns such as quoting the Bible, or bringing awareness to a cause:

> "If Guns Cause Crime, Matches Cause Arson."
>
> "The Kingdom of God is Near; Repent and Believe the Good News."

Other mottos may be geared toward politics alone, and some are indecipherable by anyone who is not a member of the group that promotes them. Whether one chooses to make a judgment, give a warning, or share some humor, slogans can have the effect of giving us an inkling about a person's beliefs, or personality. Humans seem to feel the need to communicate something to others about who they are, what they stand for, or their persona in general. Bumper stickers and T-shirts may have a momentary effect whereas specialty license plates enable citizens to further their objectives by donating to a cause, like saving the bay, supporting a charitable group, or subsidizing a benevolence fund. There are times when these efforts may form a guiding principle in life – a sort of motto for how we wish to live. In the case of license plates, displaying certain messages can influence the expectations that other drivers may come to have about one's driving behavior. What kind of driving behavior do we expect from someone displaying a rude bumper sticker? On the other hand, if someone has selected charity-based plates, is there not an expectation that they will drive more courteously?

On July 1, 2009, the Virginia General Assembly passed legislation to

> "authorize the issuance of special license plates promoting conservation on the Northern Neck, for supporters of the Shenandoah National Park Trust for its conservation efforts, and for supporters of the Choose Life Virginia Fund."

The yellow plate sporting the sketched faces of two smiling children on one side and the words "Choose Life" at the top of the plate cost approximately 60 % more than the average generic plate. The proceeds from the sale of Choose Life plates benefit state conservation efforts as well as crisis pregnancy centers, adoption agencies, and other charitable efforts to assist pregnant mothers. Drivers opting for the Choose Life plates understand their fiduciary responsibility to support their cause which generally implies the support of pro-life and other state conservation measures. Virginia is one of twenty-seven states that currently offer Choose Life license plates through the Department of Motor Vehicles.

If one were to drive a car with a Choose Life motto fixed in the front and back of the vehicle then one must be held accountable for life-affirming driving behaviors. But why stop there? Why would anyone drive more carefully and considerately in the car but behave recklessly and make careless choices in life's journeys and their daily encounters with neighbors? Do they have a responsibility to make choices that are rooted in more life-affirming concepts? It is important to remember that each decision is just a small fragment of a greater evolution of decisions, and that each choice gives life to countless new choices. Who we are and what we stand for is based on our world view and it is a direct reflection of our actions and choices.

Consider for a moment a view through a telescopic lens. If a high-powered telescope is aimed at something nearby, the view may capture an unidentifiable image, perhaps a tiny black circle surrounded by some gray matter and tiny brown flecks of different shapes and sizes. Without being able to identify the specks, the image may be deemed as insignificant. However, as the lens is adjusted to view a wider angle, the image of the tiny specks come into better focus – the gray matter with tiny black and brown flecks is now surrounded by rectangular shaped red bricks and the picture becomes clear – the telescope is aimed at a wall. By adjusting it even further, the wall may be seen as part of a fortress. If all that one observes is the tiny black speck, the big picture will never come into view. This is where many of us falter when trying to make a choice.

Frustration with the decision-making process often results from the fact that we don't possess a crystal ball; whether the decisions are simple or very complex, it is sometimes difficult to see the bigger picture. If we were able to view all possible outcomes, both now and in the future, we might possibly make very different decisions. This uncertainty can cause fear or anxiety in making a choice. Fear is a powerful dynamic that can interfere with reasonable decision-making. For example, fear can cause us to delay a decision, and that in itself is a choice that may result in an unwelcome outcome. Additionally, rethinking impulsive decisions may have favorable results. One dilemma, however, which presents itself in the decision-making process, is the need for split-second decisions. We may not always have the luxury of time to evaluate our desired outcomes, alternatives, and risks, or to ponder the bigger picture. At these times, we may rely on standard choices based on habits. If we have worked to form positive decision-making habits, our instant decisions may be more favorable. We may continue to follow the same path we have always chosen out of fear of what the other path may provide. There are times when we can benefit from the experience of others that have made certain choices, and times when we're left completely on our own.

When speaking with youngsters who talk about their place in the family, the younger siblings will often claim that they have learned a great deal by watching their older siblings. They've chosen not to do something because they've seen the consequences with their own eyes. Others, however, choose the same mistakes but rely on the notion that they can do something in a smarter way than their older siblings and not get caught. The problem with this second line of thinking is that there are usually natural consequences to many decisions and there is no way to outsmart the variables that can impact the results.

On the whole, we see that by studying history we can learn from the mistakes of our ancestors - much like older siblings who passed this way before us. And as we do with older siblings, we often judge our ancestors harshly for the mistakes they have made: behaving as barbarians, enslaving others, mandating genocides, enacting wars, claiming power as despots, supporting tyrants that subjugate human rights – and we justly criticize those who have committed unspeakable crimes against humanity. At each point along the way, it would seem that some of those figures who committed crimes against humanity had somehow managed to justify their actions in order to garner the support of a significant portion of the population. However, we can also observe that some people, perhaps in the minority, were able to see past the small speck of justification and understood the inhumane behaviors to be a destructive force of nature, and found that they had to stand up, fight against, and often die for what was inherently good. Yet today, we stand within our comfortable place in history and neglect to consider how future generations will judge us. Will our descendants applaud our lifestyles? Will they judge our civilization as being *civilized* if their inheritance is a badly damaged world or an unhealthy environment depleted of resources? Accountability is not limited to the here and now. Decision-making should not be limited to a finite view, as well. Striving to consider the bigger picture in each choice will help us to refocus those decisions which are considered to be essentially *life-giving*. If choices are directed toward the promotion of life-giving outcomes, destructive outcomes can eventually be reduced or avoided.

It is necessary to understand that there are some choices that are naturally destructive, namely those which violate human rights and freedom. Most people confuse the definitions of freedom and liberty. What is the fundamental difference between these two words and the principles for which they stand? Liberty is the sum of human rights whereas freedom is the ability of people to exercise those rights. True liberty recognizes that *life* is filled with choices, and that each person has the freedom to make choices that endow others with the freedom of choice as well. One may have the right to do something, but it doesn't make one's actions right. As guaranteed by the United States Constitution and the Bill of Rights, all citizens have a right to life, liberty and the pursuit of happiness – but within these rights and freedoms it is our responsibility to make choices that give *everyone else* the right to life, liberty and the pursuit of happiness. It is only by making life-affirming choices that future choices are permitted to grow and bear new life. Choices that place limitations on the freedom of all present and *future* citizens are choices that violate human rights. As William Allen White once said, "Liberty is the only thing you cannot have unless you give it to others."

The finite choice is one which fails to consider the bigger picture. A person may well be within their rights to exercise a freedom that justifies their needs, but without reflecting upon its societal impact, and its moral and ethical implications, the choice may be limited to thoughts of the self without exploring options that cause less harm. For example, consider the man who buys a house – he now owns the property and he is perfectly within his rights to do what he wishes. He detests the shady oak tree in the front yard so he chops it down. His next door neighbor who, over the years, nurtured hydrangeas along his own property is now faced with the destruction of his beloved plants that once thrived from the shade. Many homeowners, at one time or another, can relate to this common dilemma – when our rights to perform some action with our own property negatively affect our neighbors. We still have the right to act, but we must recognize the impact of our decisions and how harmful the results may be to others. The finite choice is one in which our decisions may cause harm that cannot be reversed or cause long-term damage that cannot be undone. Within the parameters of the finite choice, the process of life-giving options is terminated.

As seen in mathematical theory:

> "The axiom of choice asserts the existence of a choice function for any family of sets F. Suppose, however, that F is finite, or even that F just has one set. Then how do we prove the existence of a choice function? The usual answer is that we just go from set to set, picking an element from each set. Since F is finite, this process will terminate" (mathoverflow.net).

The eventuality that making selections from finite choices will be a life-giving process is contradicted by the terminal result. In math, and in life, there are no infinite possibilities where finite choices are an option. We should strive to avoid finite choices as much as we possibly can. It's important to get into the habit of making life-choices so that our central routines are based on multiple life-giving outcomes. There is sound, reasonable, logical, and even mathematical evidence to support the idea that habits that are rooted in finite decisions eventually limit our options.

Life thoughts

The best possible way to optimize ever-increasing options and the likelihood of modifications is to make the choice that does not terminate future choices.

The Nature of Choice

There is a little-known fable about a farmer who owned a moderate tract of land and planted only one crop. The soil was good for raising skirret, a perennial vegetable that could provide well for his family. The farmer had studied all he could about growing skirret and purchased an abundance of seeds to start his crops. He nurtured the soil, tended the crops and irrigated the land as needed. The land was lush and fertile and his crops grew abundantly. The farmer taught his son to water the plants, cultivate the soil and bring in the harvest. Many years later the old farmer died and his son took over the farm. He farmed the land as he'd been taught and seemed to be doing everything right, but a drought came along and the crops became sparse. The land decreased in fertility, the crops dwindled but the farmer kept on because this was all he knew how to do, and in turn he taught his own son to do the same. Eventually, the second farmer grew old and died and his son took over. One year, terrible floods came along and washed away the crops. By the time the floods ceased, the livelihood of the family had been wiped out. The young farmer looked about the wasteland and didn't know what to do. He didn't know about the seeds.

Like the old fable about the skirret farmers, performing certain actions without a core understanding of their origins and benefits can lead to a diminished set of standards that eventually weaken our cultural integrity. We know we have freedom of choice; we understand that some decisions are bad for us personally, and we can sometimes rationalize our way through decisions we know to be harmful but have deemed as the right choice. Tracing our way back to the root of what is good is essential in understanding why certain choices are inherently good, and why others are fundamentally bad.

Professor emeritus of theology and ethics at Fuller Seminary, Lewis B. Smedes, has often written on the nature of faith, God, and how human life should be lived. In his book, *My God and I: A Spiritual Memoir*, Smedes attests to the importance of extending our understanding of the human connection to God.

> "I assumed, first of all, that God the Father is the origin of all morality. If there were no God, there would be no morality, because nothing would be intrinsically right or wrong. Without God, we would probably create social conventions and social rules that might keep people from putting their hands on our purses or around our throats. But this is self-protection born of self-interest, and, while it may be practical, it does not have much to do with what is morally right and morally wrong."

Without God's moral laws, it's quite possible that we can only govern our behavior with regard to self-preservation. The result is that we don't want to break a law because we don't want to go to jail. But, if there were no jails, could we then loosen the strings that tie us to a moral code? Smedes suggests that morality should have an end, a clear objective other than self-interest, and calls upon the love and care of others as a model. His contention is firmly rooted in the concept that caring for and loving others is a two part commitment: saying no to wrong choices, and saying yes to choices that are helpful to humanity.

If one rejects the idea of moral laws as an intrinsic part of our human nature because the very idea of God is implausible, it is likely that the self-guided right and wrong principle may fall victim to relativism, where different people with different ideas of right and wrong will continually bump into each other with a series of escalating conflicts from which no one will enjoy a measure of peace no matter how right or wrong they may be. The upshot of morality is that moral laws exist as a part of creation as much as any other part of creation exists in the natural world.

"Certain natural laws exist – like physics – we don't make these laws, we discover them, we explain them" (Gerald Mann). Like many other laws in the universe, moral law, as a product of creation, is subject to specific consequences. Moral laws are woven into the fabric of life just as the laws of physics, by their own nature, keep life in the universe in place. We can defy gravity with the aid of science but we cannot obliterate it. Science can explain the laws of the universe but it cannot change them. Similarly, moral laws are meant to keep our existence in harmony with one another. We can defy moral law but we cannot escape the consequences. A person can make the choice to break with morality by living a self-indulgent or harmful lifestyle, but he cannot indefinitely escape the consequences. If, as a human race, we should suddenly decide to obliterate moral laws, would we presume that the consequences would disappear?

Moral laws have always been present and should be respected quite simply because the human persons to which they apply should be respected – in this mutual understanding of respect, harmony is to be found. In addition to carrying a physical DNA which holds the codes of our physical makeup, people have been programmed with a moral code to protect us from complete destruction, and unlike other living things we have been given a conscience to caution us about doing this kind of harm. To be fully human is to embrace every aspect of our humanity. By understanding the "moral DNA" which we all possess, we can live up to the responsibility to treat ourselves with the highest degree of respect. Living in denial of this moral DNA is tantamount to living in denial of our physical DNA. Both forms of rejection can cause us harm.

In 1962, C.S. Lewis wrote about his insights on natural law in *The Abolition of Man.* He explains:

> "It is in Man's power to treat himself as a mere 'natural object' and his own judgments of value as raw material for scientific manipulation to alter at will. The objection

> to his doing so does not lie in the fact that this point of view (like one's first day in a dissecting room) is painful and shocking till we grow used to it. . . . The real objection is that if man chooses to treat himself as raw material, raw material he will be: not raw material to be manipulated, as he fondly imagined, by himself, but by mere appetite, that is, mere Nature, in the person of his de-humanized Conditioners. . ."

Failure to recognize the complete human with both physical and moral codes decreases our full human potential, and as Lewis declares, it is *dehumanizing.* Identifying the properties of our physical codes requires eyesight, whereas recognizing the moral codes within us necessitates insight. With the aid of modern science we have been able to see the most minute characteristics of our physical being under a microscope from our cells and tissues, to our own DNA. Who we are as a physical human being can be detected by these scientific marvels. We may discover cancerous tissue as the result of making decisions to smoke cigarettes, or being exposed to other carcinogenic elements. But DNA and tissue samples fall short of revealing who we are as living beings with thoughts, ideas, behaviors, and spiritual desires to connect with our Creator.

The science of psychology has developed methods of labeling our behaviors and discovering reasons for our actions but it doesn't always give us the full picture. If we were somehow able to put our character under a microscope, what would we see? Various aspects of our personalities might come to light if we could analyze our decision-making construct. What would our moral tissues reveal about us? If there were a visible, scientific way to analyze our character, we might view individual choices as "cells" and that the fabric of our being is constructed of the sum of those choices that we have made in the past. As a person may follow healthy physical habits to enhance the quality of life, a person may also make choices for the health of their character which may find growth by routinely gravitating toward life-giving choices. How can we become more harmonized with the laws of nature that lead to humanitarian rather than egocentric choices? In treating our human selves as physical creatures only, we have severed a very important part of what makes us completely human.

As the highest form of life on the planet, humans are not only a part of nature, we also work to learn and understand it. Our desires, not necessarily *needs*, often present us with discord in living with the laws of nature. C. S. Lewis explains that man's conquest over nature comes at a hefty price, "... what we call Man's power over Nature turns out to be a power exercised by some men over other men with Nature as its instrument." In attempting to circumvent or overpower natural laws, we merely relinquish the power of our humanness. As humans with the gift of choice, we have opted to relinquish part of our humanity in order to control or dominate nature. In doing so, we have given many forms of science the power over, not only our physical humanness, but our moral humanness as well. In modern medicine, physicians, in conjunction with pharmaceutical companies, control the path of healing, reproduction, and what constitutes well-being. Bio-technology used to genetically engineer food determines the value of the food we eat. Advanced biological, scientific and technological weaponry has the potential to annihilate life on the planet. The overuse of fossil fuels is having a destructive impact on climate changes and on our health. And the list goes on. While a great many scientific advances have noticeably improved the quality of life, it is up to our human moral codes to decipher which of those advances benefit life, and which have the potential to destroy it. It is time to take a more serious look at our small, individual choices that lay the foundation for these much larger choices.

It is only when we understand and respect the laws of nature, work with them instead of against them, and implement our complete humanness for making life-giving choices, that we achieve the very best of our own human nature. In achieving this vital understanding it is important for us to recognize the non-life-giving characteristics of our own nature which constitute a base level of humanity whereby we seem prone to often make a choice against life. At times, when humanity worked toward this understanding of our weaknesses instead of away from it, it succeeded in establishing laws to deal with the injustice of self-destructive behaviors. These behaviors, if left unchecked, cause tremendous societal conflict, because we're not all on the same page. The natural choice is the one which promotes life. We have a core understanding of what appears natural and unnatural – when a mother holds her child close, nurtures, guides and defends the child, we see these as natural acts. But when a mother puts her children into a car and drives the car off a bridge to drown the children, we view this as a completely unnatural act, and worthy of punishment. Often, out of desperation, come the most destructive choices. Regardless of the degree to which one aspires to an understanding of moral law, there is an innate understanding of what is truly right and what is truly wrong, what seems natural and what seems unnatural. The time has come for us to reclaim our humanness in its totality – with regard to natural laws, morals, ethics and the ultimate goodness of the human person – not by excusing behavior, affixing blame, or by redefining something bad as something good, but by the empowerment that comes with choosing life as a natural choice.

Life thoughts

Understanding the core principles of good, life-affirming choices means that we have a reverence and respect for nature in general, and for human nature. We can rescue humanity by recognizing our greatest potentials as part of the natural world. As humans, we have a tremendous power to create and promote life, but this power comes with a great responsibility to choose life over destructive choices. The ability to examine our choices, the patterns and routines to which they are frequently subjected, and carefully integrating our capability to choose life over detrimental outcomes helps to develop our full human potential above that of other species. We can strive for the best possible us by understanding the role we play in nature.

A Vital Ingredient

In his notable book, *Emotional Intelligence: Why it Can Matter More Than IQ*, Daniel Goleman explores a fundamental aspect of our humanity: the capacity to love. He begins his work by discussing the unselfish love that a parent feels toward a child that is often demonstrated in acts of self-sacrifice:

> "As an insight into the purpose and potency of emotions, this exemplary act of parental heroism testifies to the role of altruistic love – and every other emotion we feel – in human life. It suggests that our deepest feelings, our passions and longings, are essential guides, and that our species owes much of its existence to their power in human affairs. That power is extraordinary: Only a potent love – the urgency of saving a cherished child – could lead a parent to override the impulse for personal survival. Seen from the intellect, their self-sacrifice was arguably irrational; seen from the heart, it was the only choice to make."

The basis for Goleman's book is an intense analysis of managing our emotions by use of the intellect. Unlike other living creatures, the human person exhibits an inherent power to love ourselves, beyond the limitations of self-preservation, and to love others without regard for risks. While other animals may possess characteristics that exemplify love, such as loyalty and nurturing, humans benefit from a wider range of capabilities that extend to the care and nurturing of all things. But the extent of our human capability to love is dependent upon choice. We may choose to be loyal or disloyal, caring or neglectful, charitable or selfish, and so on. The intellect is the compass we tend to rely upon in order to navigate our fluctuating emotions from one minute to the next. It is through the use of intellect that we distinguish between the choice to love and the choice to withhold love.

Goleman references *Nichomachean Ethics* when he goes on to examine the Aristotelian perspective: He writes on Aristotle's philosophical enquiry into virtue, character, and the good life…

> "Our passions, when well-exercised, have wisdom; they guide our thinking, our values, our survival. But they can easily go awry, and do so all too often. As Aristotle saw, the problem is not with emotionality, but with the *appropriateness* of emotion and its expression. The question is, how can we bring intelligence to our emotions – and civility to our streets and caring to our communal life?"

In attempting to answer this question, it is important to understand the connection between our capacity to love and our capability to make life-giving choices. It would be very difficult for one to render life-affirming choices, or to provide opportunities for growth and human development, without a certain degree of love for anyone but oneself.

When it comes to making sound choices that can benefit our lives and those of others, what is our primary motivation? Discerning the desired outcome of our choices seems to rest on the principle that our actions will result in improving our present conditions. An accepted theory is that at root of all human behavior is the desire for happiness. This ever-elusive ambition is often at the mercy of at least two variables: our impulsive choices that may be advantageous or detrimental, and well thought-out decisions do not necessarily guarantee happiness. Making choices that enable us to feel happy is difficult enough, but trying to make choices that will benefit the entire human race seems impossible to say the least. And quite frankly, what is our motivation to try to make the world happy when quite often the best we can hope for is to survive the evil that exists within it? Happiness, then, becomes a personal goal and rarely do human beings consider the idea of striving for global happiness. We've learned over time you can't make everyone happy.

In his *Nichomachean Ethics,* ancient Greek philosopher Aristotle wrote that "Every art or applied science, and every systematic investigation, and similarly every action and choice seem to aim at some good, therefore, has been well defined as that at which all things aim." This suggests that even our wrong decisions, our destructive choices and our failures, all had as a premise the need to achieve some good, even if the good was misguided or ill-conceived. Therefore, we continue to try to rectify our actions in order to achieve the good, which in theory, should lead to happiness.

Aiming for the ideology of *what is good for me is what will ultimately result in my own happiness* has certain limitations once "what is good for me" encounters disastrous results because of its effect on others. If each of the 6,840,507,003 people currently living on the planet Earth worked strictly to satisfy individual needs and achieve only personal happiness, they would soon find their efforts to be unrealistic and in the end, unsuccessful because they would constantly be bumping into someone else's efforts to do the same. Happiness, as most humans well know, is not achieved by satisfying only our own needs and those of the moment. If it were, the effort would be quite laborious and the results quite fleeting.

Aristotle derived his *Nichomachean Ethics* from an understanding of that intrinsic code of moral law.

> "Happiness is one of the most divine things, even if it is not god-sent but attained through virtue and some kind of learning or training... Activities in conformity with virtue constitute happiness, and the opposite activities constitute its opposite."

This concept brings us back to the idea of forming routines based on virtue, getting into the habit of making a choice that aims for the goodness of life. When one is confronted by the "ordinary event" one can respond by making choices from established habits or routines that are based on virtues. By applying the standard of Aristotle's ethics, humans can create a life-plan based on wisdom and understanding, charity and self-control as a means to justice.

Justice makes us happy – when our needs are heard and understood and when we find ourselves the recipients of charity we enjoy a measure of happiness that exceeds that which we can provide for ourselves alone. By the same token, as benefactors of charity to others, we may experience unprecedented and unexpected joy. Giving of ourselves adds a measure of joy to our decisions. Exercising self-control as a way to reduce conflict, excess, bitterness, anxiety, fear, and other forms of harmful behavior can bring us closer to the harmony which springs from the well of justice. Behavior born of virtue is consistent with moral law; it is that code written into our humanness which we often ignore in favor of a different standard of happiness, one which looks to momentary satisfaction, where we frantically scramble to fulfill primordial needs that keep us from achieving the highest level of our humanness. The beauty of the complete human being is seen in one who achieves an unrestricted level of charity. Achieving this level of completeness is founded on life-giving rather than destructive choices. It is through life-giving choices that we progress toward being our very best. When our motives are focused on our personal desired outcomes alone, there is no virtue in that. A squirrel desires no more than to gather nuts for his own benefit. Humans have the ability to achieve more than that.

Striving for progress based exclusively on the desire for personal happiness can often prove to be elusive because of the nature of this fleeting emotion. Daniel Goleman's thesis outlines the human advantage of being able to analyze and understand our own emotions. According to Goleman's emotional competencies, one should be able to:

- identify and name one's emotional states and understand the link between emotions, thought and action;

- to manage one's emotional states — to control emotions or to shift undesirable emotional states to more adequate ones;
- to enter into emotional states associated with a drive to achieve and be successful;
- to be sensitive to and influence other people's emotions;
- to enter and sustain satisfactory interpersonal relationships. (*Emotional Intelligence*).

Emotions can protect us, but they can also harm us. Having a clear and functional understanding of the emotional influence on decision-making can be a vital step in making better choices. Certain emotions can be catalysts for making destructive choices. While fear and anxiety are innate emotions that can caution us to make more careful choices, considering other factors such as understanding, reason, and temperance may help to balance the choices made on impulse that may prove to be harmful. Feelings such as jealousy, vengefulness, indifference, greed, and pettiness may motivate our decisions but it can be very difficult to make life-giving choices. At times our mindset may result in hasty decisions that are irreparable. Applying the intellect to understand and manage these types of emotions, those that we all experience from time to time, can better aid us to make sound judgments that can steer us in a more restorative direction. The intellect may be guided by the desire to grow and expand our choices rather than reduce and limit them, by preferring the habit to love rather than to be guided by hate.

The great Roman orator, Marcus Tullius Cicero, outlined the four aspects of love which clearly delineate its varying natures and the forms it takes in relationships. At the most basic level, the easiest and first aspect of love is *cupiditas* which refers to desire. This first type of love seeks self-gratification. It desires to possess that which will gratify the needs of the self. It is not necessarily concerned with the needs of the other person, nor does it give life to the relationship. This type of "love" can exist as a form of desire alone, wishing to gratify base needs and without a care for what happens next. Desire is a healthy emotion, but alone and without growth potential, it's restrictive.

The second form of love is known as the *eros* or romantic love where the focus is still somewhat on the self – this is what you can do for *me*. Romantic love is exemplified by phrases like *I feel good when I'm with you. I love the way you make me happy.* In essence it can involve acts of mutual self-gratification. This type of love, romantic in its ideals, has limitations because until one gives selflessly, growth in the relationship is incomplete. This kind of relationship, when it reaches the stage of *this isn't working for me*, finds that the relationship may come to an end. When the going gets tough someone will bail out.

The third type of love is known as familial love or *amicitia*. This type of love is based on loving someone for who they are. This is a mutual bond of understanding which one finds in friendship. One begins to let go of their own needs in favor of the other person, to be there for them, to support them through difficulties, serious illness, and crises. This love allows for the opening of one's heart for the benefit of others. This type of love is found in close relationships with family and friends and can often weather many storms for the duration which makes it much more life-giving than the lower forms of "love."

Finally, Cicero spoke of the highest form of love – *agape* – a type of love that is not only selfless but sacrificial. It is the type of love that's going to cost you something. One is willing to love for the sole benefit of another. This is the highest form of love because it requires the most from us as human beings. It is the mother who is willing to give up her own life and her own needs for the good of her children. It is the father who makes daily sacrifices to care for his family. It is the soldier who goes into battle and is willing to die for the sake of freedom of people he doesn't even know. It is the firefighter or police officer that day-in and day-out is willing to put his/her life on the line for the higher good. It is the nurse who sits with a dying patient after her shift has finished. Sacrifice is something humanity still respects; we honor the men and women who have given their lives for others by showing some form of gratitude and admiration.

This highest form of love we have witnessed on many levels, as in the love of God or Christ for all of humanity. In the New Testament, Jesus of Nazareth said, "Greater love has no one than this, that he lay down his life for his friends" (John 15:13). We see it as covenant love of God for his creation, and again he reminds us "To love one another as I have loved you" (John 13:34). This is the expectation – that we love one another by *giving life*, our own lives, for the sake of another. This kind of love is unconditional and doesn't fall short of ultimate sacrifice. It is the greatest life-giving form of love. When see the highest form of love we will see the highest quality choice that one can make. When making choices, we may ask, "At what level of love is this choice based upon?"

What would the world be like if not one human being ever rose above the level of *cupiditas*? If each and every human being never loved anyone but himself or herself, what kind of a world would we live in? It is safe to assume that it could degenerate into something less than human. To be fully human is to love to our highest potential, not only for family and friends, but for strangers as well. At the very least, politeness is required when dealing with others. Polite behavior gives life, whereas rude behavior is destructive. *I'm going to give up my poor attitude to give someone a kinder part of me.* When we encounter people in traffic, or in crowded shopping areas or in work environments consider what a consistent rude pattern of behavior provokes in others versus a more respectful approach. If we treat everyone with kindness and respect, we are nurturing a life-giving blue-print for better living. Again, Jesus sent us a clear message "For if you love those who love you, what reward have you?" (Matthew 5:43-46)

This philosophy brings us back to virtue. What is at the core of our humanity? What makes us truly human? *Virtus* in Latin means worth - for people to be entirely human, their worth must be valued. It is an unhealthy society that doesn't recognize the value of being human and degrades its worth. On some level we understand this; as a nation we have gone to war against despots who violate human rights. But we need to understand this on all levels. We need to put the worth of the human being into every aspect of life. This valuation begins with a number of actions that promote life rather than destroying it.

One of the most widely used readings incorporated into wedding ceremonies is St. Paul's letter to the people of Corinth when he defined the very essence of love as a way to counsel them on moral responsibility.

The commonly known "Way of Love" is not advice for married couples alone but a study on how the act of truest love (which can be found between two people) may be applied to the greater society by virtue of our human kinship.

> "If I speak in the tongues of men and of angels, but have not love, I am a noisy gong or a clanging cymbal. And if I have prophetic powers, and understand all mysteries and all knowledge, and if I have all faith, so as to remove mountains, but have not love, I am nothing. If I give all I have, and if I deliver my body to be burned, but have not love, I gain nothing.
>
> Love is patient, love is kind; love does not envy, it does not boast, it is not proud. It is not rude, it is not self-seeking; it is not easily angered, it keeps no record of wrongs. Love does not delight in evil but rejoices in the truth. Love bears all things, believes all things, hopes all things, endures all things" (1 Corinthians 13:1-7).

It is evident that St. Paul's description of love amounts to a great deal more than a passing emotion. It is a way of *living.* To live one's life according to this understanding of the nature of love requires that one must aspire to be the best person that one can be, and to aim for the highest choices that bear the fruits of life – the very choices that necessitate love. Patience and kindness have a way of extending the life of love. In contrast, behaviors that are jealous, boastful, proud, rude, self-seeking, anger-driven, resentful, or just plain *evil* are not life-giving behaviors. In order to choose life, to choose the path of goodness, love is a pre-requisite. St. Paul is clear, without love, all good intentions amount to nothing because they lack growth potential. Love is the most essential component in making choices that give value to life. Being fully-human means we possess and utilize all the qualities that engender love and we have the aptitude for higher decision-making and the capability to choose life. By exercising this capability in unison with one another, humanity has the power to exert boundless loving kindness. We cannot make life-giving choices without love.

Life thoughts

Giving freely of ourselves and presenting our talents, works, skills and assistance to one another is a choice made of love. Life is a wonderful gift and love makes it all the more wonderful. Love is not a feeling; it is a choice to act, to give, and to nurture life. Wherever love is the choice in life-decisions there is a continuation of life. If we remove love from our decisions, some part of life suffers or is irrevocably damaged.

The Decision-Making Hierarchy

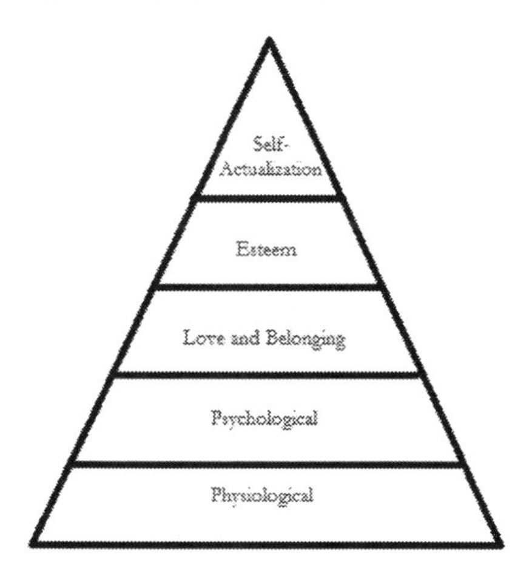

In 1943, Abraham Maslow wrote a paper entitled "The Theory of Motivation" after studying people he called *exemplary*. His famous theory is most commonly recognized in the hierarchy of human needs and is most often seen as a pyramid. At the bottom of the pyramid Maslow illustrates that our primary motivation is rooted in satisfying our physical needs. We are governed by the laws of nature which compel us to achieve homeostasis by breathing, eating, drinking, sleeping, procreating, and excreting waste. These constitute our most basic human needs and a fundamental sort of happiness depends on their fulfillment. If one is homeless, starving and destitute, it is more difficult, or unlikely that he or she will be considering how to make choices that benefit humanity. We must satisfy certain needs in order to work toward the upper levels of Maslow's hierarchy by fostering behaviors that help us grow as humans for our own benefit and the benefit of the human race.

The second level in Maslow's hierarchy emphasizes the psychological need for safety and security. Once the lower physiological needs have been met, people generally concentrate on self-preservation, to be kept from harm, to promote well-being and secure their necessary resources. With the realization of these first two levels of vital needs, humans then search for love and belonging through relationships with family and with friends. A person can become preoccupied with satisfying any of these three lower levels of basic needs and remain here rather than progressing to the higher levels of the pyramid which focus on esteem and self-actualization – or in other words, the complete human being. People make hundreds of choices at each level of Maslow's hierarchy, but how can we ensure that these choices are life-giving? For the most part the human population has the ability in the course of their daily circumstances to utilize the choose life motto to maximize their highest human potential at each level.

Physiological Choices

Water, Food and Rest – While everyone has a basic need for food, water, and rest, we have found that getting all the food we can possibly eat, sleeping most of the day away, or drinking to satisfy an unquenchable thirst does not necessarily make us a better person, nor does it make us physically healthy. In their book, *The Ethics of Food Choices: Why Our Food Choices Matter*, authors Peter Singer and Jim Mason explore the "rights and wrongs" of the choices we make with regard to what we eat. One interviewee was quoted as saying, "I try to vote with my dollar and not enrich those who are doing bad things in the world." The life-giving choice to make healthier selections in what we eat is just one tiny facet of the choose life paradigm. Evidently, those who give strong consideration to eating for better living are committed to the idea that choosing life means eating healthier foods.

Amazon.com lists over 29,000 books dedicated to the theme *food choices*. Selecting foods that promote health has always been a life-giving choice whereas eating whatever we like leads to pandemic health issues and early death. That's just the way it is. We must eat, but we need to understand the difference between needs and wants. We need food to live but we may want foods that are unhealthy or more than our bodies need in order to be healthy. Water is life-sustaining and what our bodies need, yet often other beverages comprise the choices we make that replace water in our diets. These choices are based on *wants* and not necessarily *needs*. How do our wants cause us harm when we confuse them with our needs?

Nutritionists at the University of California, Berkeley, George Briggs and Doris Calloway emphasize that,

> "The foods we eat contain 42 to 44 highly important substances (the 'nutrients') that each of us must consume in adequate amounts in order to have energy, grow, reproduce, and lead a full healthy life. [These important substances include] vitamins, amino acids, fats, and probably several carbohydrates for energy and roughage… These essential nutrients provide fuel, catalysts, and machinery so that we can grow, move about, see, hear, taste, smell, feel, speak, think, learn and remember, sing, walk, run, play, enjoy pleasures, argue, make decisions, love, and be innovative and creative…. If an inadequate amount is eaten, or too much of some, these functions will be impaired. Life itself is dependent upon what we eat."

Making choices that include excess fat, sugars, and additives cause harm and these choices should not be confused with a standard of meeting our physical *needs*. There is no shortage of nutritional advice in this day and age. Without much difficulty we can become more knowledgeable about healthy, nutritional choices so that we can live a more healthy lifestyle; not just eating to satisfy hunger, but making food choices that are aimed at healthy living by choosing life-promoting options. The food industry needs an overhaul so that people can make healthier food choices that are more affordable and accessible. When the more inexpensive option consists of choices that contain harmful ingredients, then the choices made by scientists, farmers and producers, manufacturers and distributors have a tremendous impact on the choice of one individual who wishes to eat healthier but cannot afford to do so.

Here again, society is confronted with the challenge of caring for oneself as well as caring for others. When airline safety instructions are prescribed by the team of stewards prior to a flight regarding oxygen masks *passengers are instructed to make sure their masks are on first before assisting other passengers or children.* This directive is applicable to many situations in life but should never be misconstrued to focus on the self alone. Life-giving practices include taking care of ourselves *and* others. Donating processed, unhealthy foods to the poor while we dine on salmon is the equivalent of using an oxygen mask for ourselves and offering a paper bag to the next passenger. Non-perishable food selections should offer quality nutrition to those in need. We must find a way to pay life forward in all that we do.

Procreation is also a basic human need to which is attached an immeasurable number of choices. When human beings separate the idea of procreation from sex, the choices may fall into an abyss of non-life-giving decisions. Humans have a greater capacity for intimacy, expressions of love, and taking part in the life-giving force of the sexual act than diminishing its highest potential to pleasure alone. Pleasure is wonderful, but we may not see the bigger picture if we compartmentalize the act and focus primarily on limited choices and behaviors. Sexuality without life-affirming motives has not benefitted humanity. Mary Eberstadt, in her recent book entitled *Adam and Eve After the Pill: Paradoxes of the Sexual Revolution* challenges the effects of the sexual revolution and reveals the destructive aftermath. She succinctly refers to the sexual revolution as the "destigmatization and demystification of the nonmarital sex act and the reduction of sexual relations in general to a kind of hygienic recreation in which anything goes so long as those involved are consenting adults." In her noteworthy books and articles, Eberstadt makes a formidable case for the greatest casualty of the sexual revolution: children. She underscores that one of the most expressive art forms – music - to have evolved from this past generation explicitly articulates the effects of the sexual revolution on the children who were products of this cultural transformation:

> "Contemporary rock and rap, for instance, are driven in significant measure by the fallout from the sexual revolution; their predominant themes (apart from sex itself) include broken homes, broken families, mom's abusive boyfriends, sexual predators, and the rest of the revolution's effects" (from Policy Review – Eminem is Right, no. 128).

Music from any generation strongly reflects the social issues that the young must contend with and often this fact is recognized in retrospect. This past generation's rock and rap music has been vehemently rebellious. If modern culture would have everyone believe that the outcome of the free love revolution was a new sort of *freedom-paradise*, what are the young people revolting against? If the sexual revolution was the panacea to the constrictive social ills of the past, why are the themes of modern music so violently opposed to the aftermath?

Additionally, in her book, Eberstadt affirms that women are paradoxically the co-heirs of this disaster of the sexual revolution.

> "For women, though, the fallout from the revolution seems more immediate and acute. It is women who have abortions and get depressed about them, women who are left to raise children alone when a man leaves for someone else, women who typically take the biggest financial hit in divorce, and women who fill the pages of such magazines as *Cosmopolitan* and *Mirabella* and chatty websites like *Salon* with sexual doublespeak. Just look at any one of those sources --- or any random segment of women's morning talk shows or other popular 'chick' fare like the television series *Sex in the City*. All reveal a widely contradictory mix of chatter about how wonderful it is that women are now liberated for sexual fun --- and how

mysteriously impossible it has become to find a good, steady, committed boyfriend at the same time."

Eberstadt quotes a number of expert sources to make her case that the sexual revolution has done more harm than good, that by isolating the sexual act from its life-giving procreative purposes, we have created more problems that enable more destructive and non-life-giving decisions. The questions arise: Do we have a better society with fewer social problems because we have liberated the sexual act from its previously defined parameters? Have we reduced the number of violent sexual acts committed each year as a result? Have we eradicated crimes against children because we now choose when to have them? Have we become better parents and eradicated child abuse because we're more selective about having children? Are the children that come along "by accident" the only ones that are products of divorce and single-family homes, neglect, abuse, disorders, and subject to dysfunctional families? Has pornography or pedophilia diminished since the dawn of the sexual revolution? Are men happier with the sexual utopia? Are women?

Eberstadt refers to sociologist Kay S. Hymowitz when she develops her thesis on this topic and its effects on the male population: "Modern men exist in a state of suspended adolescence" and goes on to say that "men and women had unwittingly put themselves on a collision course with human nature itself." The bottom line is that while sex and procreation are fundamental human needs, they deserve the same serious attention as our other basic needs, by applying conscious life-giving choices to our conduct. If an unlimited consumption of fats, sugars and additives has led to an epidemic of life-threatening diseases, then so, too, has an unrestricted indulgence in the basic need for sex led to a threat to quality of life. While nutritionists and doctors agree that preventative measures such as healthy lifestyles, beneficial and limited eating, and getting exercise support healthy living, and that pharmaceuticals are just bandages with side effects, sociologists and researchers understand that unrestricted sexual conduct can result in unhealthy relationships, abandonment, STD's, and unwanted pregnancies, and that contraceptives, abortifacients, and abortion are the equivalent surface remedies with side effects offered as a solution.

Life-giving choices begin with the first decision to choose a healthy life path by making choices that support taking control of one's life from the most elementary level. The choose life approach to sexual decisions involves respect for who you are as a living human being; it requires an understanding of possible outcomes and an effort to avoid heartbreaking decisions down the road.

Psychological Needs - Safety and Security

Safety ranks just above physiological needs in the hierarchy of human needs. Our need to feel safe emotionally as well as physically depends largely on our understanding of what constitutes a threat to safety. Physical safety is a high priority in the wide spectrum of daily life – including our living quarters, our workplace environment, transportation, medical issues and settings, schools, recreation, national defense, as well as the safety of our food and water, and the very air we breathe. The decisions we make, as well as the decisions made by others may seriously affect the safety and security aspects of living from day to day. In almost every category where safety becomes an issue, safety-training is the first step to insuring the well-being of the population. Homes, shelters, and temporary habitats provide people with at least a moderate feeling of safety and security from the elements, predators, criminals and the like, but the abode itself must be deemed worthy of habitation.

Many government agencies have been created for the purpose of ensuring our safety. OSHA (Occupational Safety and Health Administration – a division of the US Dept. of Labor) was created by Congress in 1970 to assure the health and safety of men and women in the workplace by setting standards and offering safety training. The Department of Transportation along with the Department of Motor Vehicles works to ensure safe travels for citizens. The Food and Drug Administration, the American Medical Association, the American legal system, the United States Military, Departments of Education, and so on, comprise just a short list of the agencies and systems in place to address the human need for safety and security. All of these entities work to build a safer world, but it still remains up to individuals and the decisions we make to work in unison with these organizations to make safer choices – for ourselves and for others. For example, there is only so much the DMV can do to promote safe driving – education, testing, licensing, and addressing violations through the court system only go so far to ensure the safety of drivers. It still remains an individual choice to make safe decisions on the road by not driving aggressively or impaired, by obeying speed limits, signals, and stop signs, by showing courtesy to other drivers and not making decisions that will endanger your own life or the life of others. We all desire to live in a safer world, but our individual decisions have a greater impact on this ideology than most of us are willing to accept.

In order to make sound, healthy decisions that impact the safety and security of society as a whole, education is an imperative, as Mini Krishnan points out in her article, *Building a Safer World* writes,

> "Educating for peace seeks to nurture a moral vision about the role of the self in the family, society, nation and the world. If we are to survive on an impoverished planet that cannot manage its food-stocks or famines, its water resources or forests, we must, as quickly as possible, see ourselves as a global family and sensitize children to understand that what affects one group in one part of the world, will eventually affect everyone everywhere else. If we are to make the world a safer and better place we must also plan how to raise safer and better people. We have already learnt how to make children healthier but we have paid less attention to the hearts and minds of children. Surely the goal of education is to equip people to lead meaningful lives and not merely to make a living."

Building a safer world includes a more serious and focused attention to morality – how our actions affect others and their well-being; the protection of life and family by making choices that support the safety of children and families in all their environments, including homes, schools and workplaces and by enriching the economy so that employment and general welfare are not imperiled and that crime is not an option; by expanding resources so that life-choices are available to everyone; by looking out for one another – for their property, their health, and their safety. Building a safer world means safeguarding the idea of social responsibility by making better, life-giving choices; it begins with caring about what happens to other people as much as we care about what happens to ourselves.

Love and Belonging Choices

"We cannot escape the necessity of love and compassion." (Dalai Lama)

In relationships, life-giving choices respect the dignity of the person and strive to do no harm. By establishing a clear definition of the relationship, understanding the role that must be played, and determining the life-giving choices in words and actions can help a relationship to grow. Likewise, understanding what constitutes destructive behavior can help one avoid the pitfalls that harm a good relationship.

To begin, it is vital to have a good relationship with oneself. We know from the relationships that we maintain with others that the choices we make in the relationship can nurture the relationship, damage it, or end it. By making life-giving choices we can nurture the inner-self with care, self-respect, and seeking help if needed. Occasionally, choices that we make can damage or destroy a part of us. When we say, "I've made such a mess of things" we recognize that we could have made better choices. By making choices that devalue our humanness and the good things in our lives we cause harm that is often more far-reaching than just how it affects us personally. By treating ourselves with love and care, we grow, we love, we give life to the world rather than deplete it.

If you've ever heard someone say, "I can't trust myself" it is evident that there is something wrong, broken, or damaged within the individual. As with any other relationship, trust is a crucial component. A person who cannot trust himself has come to that realization because of experience and a history of making self-destructive choices. By driving head first into impulsive behavior in order to satisfy an immediate need or to assuage a hurt that hasn't healed one engages in lifelong patterns of behavior that will require rehabilitation and healing.

In order to create a better environment for ourselves, and by extension create a better world in which to live, the healing process must begin with each and every one of us. Changing negative behaviors into life-giving or healing patterns helps us to become more fully human, the person we were created to be. Selfish behavior, where we are only thinking of ourselves and our own needs, is not life-giving behavior. For example, if fruit is not used it begins to rot. Fruit is meant to spread its seeds, to be eaten, to be baked into something delicious. If fruit is left on its own, natural bacteria, once good for the fruit, begin to act upon it. The warmth of sunshine that encouraged growth while the fruit was still attached to the vine, now begins to cause the fruit to rot. As with humans, turning inward and remaining inward can begin a process of deterioration of the spirit. Doting on our own immediate needs, detaching ourselves or withdrawing charity from others, or concentrating on the feel-good aspect of life achieved through selfish behaviors, does not help us grow and meet our full human potential.

Family and Friends – Build something life-giving: a family, a home, a community – do this by treating each other well and by caring for one another. Life-affirming choices are integral to the growth and well-being of any relationship. There is an etiquette to healthy relationships and this etiquette is rooted in love. Ralph Waldo Emerson wrote in *The Conduct of Life*, that

> "Bad behavior the laws cannot reach. Society is infested with rude, cynical, restless, and frivolous persons who prey upon the rest... Manners are factitious, and grow out of circumstance as well as out of character... Fine manners need the support of fine manners in others. Manners require time, as nothing is more vulgar than

> haste. Friendship should be surrounded with ceremonies and respects, and not crushed into corners. Friendship requires more time than poor busy men can usually command. Society is the stage on which manners are shown."

Emerson speaks at great length about the necessity of manners in a well-developed culture. Political correctness should not take the place of manners. They are not synonymous terms. We often find that politically correct statements can devalue a person's worth as much as belligerent barbs. Manners necessitate a respect for a person's position, beliefs, and status and should never be watered-down in the interest of sterile, politically correct language that lacks genuine caring. Devaluation of life is a symptom of extreme cultural rudeness; it leaves no room for growth in family relationships, friendships, or societal involvements.

Supportive vs. enabling behavior – We cannot speak about relationships without clarifying the difference between being supportive – which promotes life-giving decisions, and enabling – which promotes destructive decisions. Psychologists agree that there is an enormous difference between these two factors which affect relationships between family members, friends, co-workers, educators, health issues, the legal system, etc…

Supportive behavior recognizes an effort on someone's part to improve their life by making better decisions, or being aware of someone's weaknesses, illness, hurt, or disability and by helping them to heal. Assisting others in need to regain autonomy is supportive. Helping students with special needs to recognize their talents and productive abilities encourages growth in ways that the disabling methods of the past never could. Support comes in a number of varieties – emotional, psychological, financial, and physical. It brings us back to the original hierarchy of human needs. Being supportive means being attentive to someone's *needs* but making certain that what the person needs is actually clear and not ambiguous and harmful. Support means to provide assistance with clear and definable boundaries. For example, a couple in their sixties that invites their forty-year-old son to move back home until he can financially get back on his feet are being supportive. If the forty-year old son remains in the home for years without assisting his parents financially or otherwise and makes the living arrangement permanent is no longer being supported, but enabled. Support means to provide assistance so that someone can grow, not become stagnant. Boundary lines are essential when establishing supportive vs. enabling behaviors.

The psychology community has addressed this issue when dealing with addictions. They have helped to define the enabler as

> "One that enables another to persist in self-destructive behavior (as substance abuse) by providing excuses or by making it possible to avoid the consequences of such behavior. When one becomes an enabler, it can be destructive to themselves, to the person (or people) being enabled, and to the people around them" (asktheinterntherapist.com).

Supportive behavior supports life by helping someone to take responsibility for their situation, while enabling behavior enables destruction by fostering some type of dependency. Programs specifically designed to help people with addictions understand this concept. They help individuals to take responsibility for their condition and provide support and a means to gain control of their own lives by teaching them to make healthier choices. Making excuses for bad decisions does not promote growth; it enables a pattern of bad decision-making behavior. Understanding the root of bad decisions is the first step toward accountability and change. Providing support when growth is the goal is a life-giving practice, while supplying a crutch when dependency is the outcome is the enabling alternative. The premise of supportiveness may be applied to relationships as well as societal, economic and political goals. All those that play key roles in the advancement of family issues as well as socio-economic concerns should work to reevaluate the desired goals for the life we share on this planet.

Esteem

Self-esteem, confidence, and self-respect are characteristics that are built through consistent efforts to better our lives. Obeying laws, not because we fear the consequences but because it's the right thing to do builds character. Discerning the value of a law requires that we apply the same principles as we do to human life by examining the laws of nature and the laws of morality. Showing self-restraint and self-discipline is a life-giving practice because we recognize that our rights end where the rights of another person begin. We may have the right to commit an act, but it doesn't make the act right. We have the right to free speech but we do not have the right to use that freedom to destroy another person's character. We have the right to bear arms but we do not have the right to take a life unlawfully. We have the right to life, liberty and the pursuit of happiness. This is our most fundamental right. We do not have the right to destroy life, to destroy liberty, or to destroy one's happiness. We must work to ensure that we pass on these fundamental rights to all of humanity. We build our esteem by respecting these vital human rights and by defending them if they should become threatened.

Self-esteem and confidence can be achieved through bettering our circumstances, through education, hard work, diligence and living life by applying the principle of Choose Life in every aspect. Choose life in your career choice – jobs that promote life and well-being can include anything from food service to peace ambassador. Give life to the world by doing your job for the good of humanity. Construction is constructive, teaching is advancing knowledge, protecting and serving safeguards human worth. Esteem in medicine should be life-giving according to the Hippocratic Oath, particularly as it states:

> "I will apply, for the benefit of the sick, all measures required, avoiding those twin traps of overtreatment and therapeutic nihilism. I will remember that there is art to medicine as well as science, and that warmth, sympathy, and understanding may outweigh the surgeon's knife or the chemist's drug… Most especially must I tread

> with care in matters of life and death. If it is given to me to save a life, all thanks. But it may also be within my power to take a life; this awesome responsibility must be faced with great humbleness and awareness of my own frailty. Above all, I must not play at God… I will remember that I remain a member of society with special obligations to all my fellow human beings, those sound of mind and body as well as the infirm. If I do not violate this oath, may I enjoy life and art, be respected while I live and remembered with affection thereafter. May I always act so as to preserve the finest traditions of my calling and may I long experience the joy of healing those who seek my help."

The message of the Hippocratic Oath is a professional approach to preserving the quality and dignity of human life. However, this oath is of value in any profession: to respect the life of the people you work with and for whom you are responsible. Educators are often reminded of their responsibility by the gifts they sometimes receive from students – some type of mug or plaque that depicts the message *Teachers Touch the Future.* One might add to that: *Be very careful how you touch their future.*

To perform every task in life with goodness, honor and respect validates and justifies our humanness. Esteem is not pride – not in the sense that pride can destroy value. Esteem is lifting our efforts up to the heights of our talents, good fortune, and grace. Esteem is the way we show appreciation for these gifts and we recognize worth: our own worth and its benefit to the human race. Esteem can also include a sense of humility – whereby we always struggle to do something just a little bit better than we did before and recognizing the talents, fortune and grace that others possess. We are all working together for the good of humankind. Esteem helps us to see our role in this effort; humility helps us to keep things in perspective, that we are just one small part of the big picture. As individuals we are challenged to imagine *all possibilities* as a way out of hardship and struggles, that perhaps what is difficult may be what is best for us, to be able to say "I love myself enough not to make a choice that will leave me feeling devastated and without life-giving options."

Self-Actualization

The term *self-actualization* has most people stumped – what on earth does it mean? It is a step up from *self-esteem* and most people agree that self-esteem means you feel good about yourself, or you have a good self image. While self-esteem may be accomplished unrealistically through self-indulgence, one may feel good about oneself without a clear and viable basis for doing so. True esteem stems from the fortitude required to improve one's conditions in life by increasing the efforts to better the world and humanity as well.

Self-actualization means to become actual. In other words – that self-esteem exists in the *act* and not merely in the *potential.* Self-actualization exists in reality at the highest level of our humanness. At the stage of self-actualization we *act* to serve the greater good – this is a level of achievement that synchronizes all our behaviors to reflect our core values. Among the characteristics of self-actualization is creativity. As humans we have the power to create, but again we are faced with choices. Self-actualization requires the greatest level of responsibility, for ourselves and for the world around us. A choice which improves the self by creating widespread benefits for communities and society is self-actualizing in the greatest sense of the term, while creating an environment that is harmful or destructive is not utilizing creativity for life-giving possibilities. Creativity can generate possibilities for countless new and revitalizing choices that work within the spirit of life energy. Problem solving is another aspect of self-actualization and is obviously held to the same life-affirming criteria. Productivity necessitates creative and industrious problem-solving skills that take the laws of nature, moral and ethical laws into account. Problem-solving techniques that end life, destroy possibilities, or crush the human spirit have an overall detrimental property that is non-productive.

Complacency works against self-actualization. There is value in recognizing "This is who I am, accept me. I love the way I am." But, if these attitudes inhibit growth and one doesn't see opportunities to improve it is stagnation that benefits no one, especially not oneself.

Ironically, once we reach the stage of self-actualization the hierarchy of human needs becomes inverted. One is no longer concerned primarily with the *self*; the truly self-actualized individual no longer places a tremendous emphasis on one's own bottom-level needs to the point of obscuring the needs of others, nor can one conceive of the idea of placing one's own welfare above the greater good. At this stage, there is a well-defined proportionality constant in which one cares for the self as a member of the whole, and cares for the whole as a greater part of the self. Self-actualization diminishes the tremendous weight one places on satisfying one's needs of the moment and concentrates on the bigger picture without excluding the core principle: that life is the greater choice above personal needs. The hierarchy is then seen in reverse:

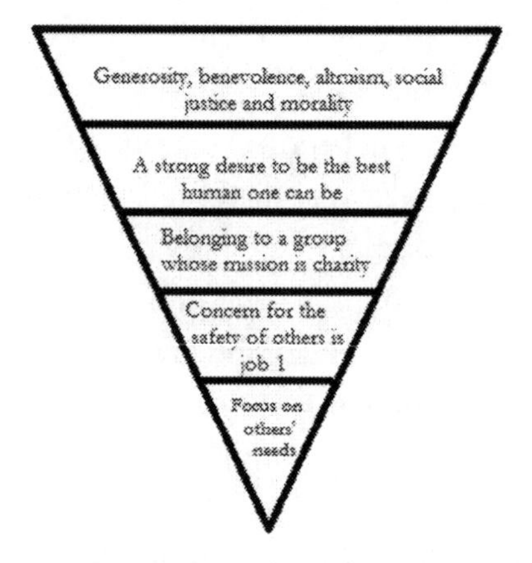

All actions are choices. At this level of decision-making, one's actions may result from consistent life-giving choices that not only benefit the self but support humanity as well. It is a pathway that helps the individual to be the best human he/she can be and benefits humanity so that we all can be the best we can be, not only by decisions, but by visible examples and consequences. There have been notable people who have demonstrated this type of moral courage and a strong desire to benefit humanity above one's own personal needs, such as: Nelson Mandela, Martin Luther King, Jr., Mahatma Ghandi, Oskar Schindler, Irena Sendler, Mother Teresa, Francis of Assisi, just to name a few, who chose peaceful and *life-giving* means of exacting the changes they wished to see in the world around them – life-giving because their actions brought new life into the world and led the way by example by using their special, self-actualized talents for good and not for destruction, division, and death. We admire these examples, not only because of their individual chosen paths but because of their contributions to humanity – in essence, they have given the human race a good name having reached a level of self-actualization to which we can aspire and appreciate. The key is to strike a balance where the best life-giving choice is achieved through unity and peace. Though, as we have seen throughout history and in current times, there are occasions when tyrants do not respond to peaceful measures, or times when leaders feel the need to divide and conquer their population with refined rhetoric - these measures may be directed toward change, but division is discord, and schisms are not known to be life-giving forces. There can be no true justice without the life-supporting work. The highest level of humanity demands that we work for justice, and for the betterment of life, not only for ourselves but for everyone through unity and peace. Making life-choices entails an understanding that *all life* must benefit from our decisions, not only our own but everyone and everything. This fundamental principle does not exclude the value of any human life; it respects the significance of how each facet of life (*humans, animals, plants, resources, energy*) fit together to encompass the larger picture of life on the planet Earth. Each component of life, no matter how large or how small, is integral to the functionality of the whole. All life matters; all matter has life-value.

Life thoughts

As human beings we have every right to make choices that satisfy our basic needs. It is a privilege to have the free will to choose, not only what we need, but what we want. Needing and wanting are not wrong. How we choose to satisfy those needs and wants can be loving or destructive. Everything we do begins with a choice. We have the responsibility to make choices that fulfill our desires in a humanly responsible way. When we overindulge in gratifying our basic human needs, we are no longer making life-affirming choices; we are taking something away from life.

The Tools We Need to Make Life-Giving Choices

An idea whose time has come once again: *One should treat others in a way in which one would like to be treated*, once avidly known as the Golden Rule, it is now an affirmation that requires a new perspective. This rule is fundamentally reciprocal and cannot foster goodness in a one-sided arena; we want to be treated well therefore we must treat others well. It's easy to misconstrue this rule by treating others as we have been treated, which isn't always in a loving manner. As all people would like to be treated with kindness, dignity and respect, they must in turn use these virtues to guide the manner in which they treat others and every facet of life on the planet. This reciprocity has all the earmarks of life-sustaining choices, but we often forget what those choices may be. Every word we speak, every action we take finds its root in our routine thought processes.

Margaret Thatcher, the longest serving Prime Minister of the United Kingdom, is said to have quoted an unknown author when she said:

> "Watch your thoughts for they become words. Watch your words for they become actions. Watch your actions for they become habits. Watch your habits, for they become your character. And watch your character, for it becomes your destiny! What we think we become."

Louise Hay, inspirational author, lecturer and teacher of personal growth and healing methods, has motivated millions of people worldwide with her concentrated messages of restoring our health through positive thinking. Hay writes,

> "Moment by moment, we're consciously or unconsciously choosing healthy thoughts or unhealthy thoughts. These thoughts affect our bodies. One thought by itself doesn't have much influence over us. However, we all think more than 60,000 thoughts a day, and the effect on our thoughts is cumulative. Poisonous thoughts poison our bodies. Science is now confirming that we can't allow ourselves to indulge in negative thinking. It's making us sick and it's killing us."

What we think is what we become and what we become affects the entire human race. Habits of ego-centrism make it very difficult to genuinely speak and act in a way that gives life to the world around us. As with any tools, a rudimentary understanding of the desired end result can better enable one to use life-giving tools properly. The tools needed to make life-giving choices begin with understanding our own thoughts, how those thoughts translate into our actions and routines, and the impact these actions have on others. As a result, we come to understand this progression because of how we feel when we are the target of actions perpetrated by others as a result of their own thoughts. When considering the outcomes of destructive choices versus the effects of life-giving choices, it is important to remember that how we treat ourselves is as critical as how we treat others. We must always strive to attain a balance between nurturing the self and cultivating goodness in the world around us.

Among the tools needed to make more humanitarian choices are well-developed emotional, as well as intellectual, maturity, and a foundation of love. Behaviors that are reactive rather than reflective can be injurious. Thoughts and actions that foster prejudices, anger, dependency, negativism, self-indulgence and bullying are characteristically immature behaviors. Achieving a higher level of humanness necessitates growth beyond such behaviors. This construct leads to social maturity where one feels more comfortable reflecting on one's circumstances and making the life-giving choices based on the golden rule rather than group conformity to the influence of pop culture. Actions rooted in reflective thought, love, and moral laws are well-established in the guiding principles of life. These actions are directed toward the betterment of life for one and for all; they are the energy force that pushes humanity forward, even if setbacks occur because of passing trends.

Throughout history, we have witnessed examples when certain ideas and thoughts were implemented as a way to improve the quality of life for some people or select group without regard for the value of *all* human life. Because certain practices were accepted by a majority, they were deemed suitable for society. Some commonly accepted ideas of the past that were promoted for the well-being of society but were not life-giving in nature included, but are not limited to:

- The custom in ancient cultures, including the highly civilized Greek and Roman cultures with regard to their treatment of infants and children born with physical or mental disabilities or were simply born of the wrong gender were abandoned to the elements and left to die. Philo of Alexandria was the first to speak out against this common practice.
- At numerous points throughout history, slavery was an accepted practice as far back as 1760 BC. Once societies and operative social units were formed, slavery became necessary when labor was in short supply. CNN reports that slavery continues to plague the country of Mauritania decades after it was abolished by law because it is still overlooked for political, religious, racist and other reasons. (http://www.cnn.com)
- The development of nuclear weaponry was supported as a means to advance war technology. Though many have

recognized the destructive possibilities of nuclear arms, they continue to exist and pose a threat to life on this planet.

As we can see from this short list, many ideas throughout history that were commonplace, supported by the progressive thinking of the time, encouraged and accepted for the common good, were not necessarily practices that valued the goodness of life. While the practice of eliminating disabled or unwanted infants was progressive in the sense that survival of the species was a desired outcome, it led to thoughts of ethnic cleansing and intolerance for individuals with special needs; whereas slavery was considered to be economically feasible for society, it was an abhorrent practice that was catastrophic to human dignity. Ironically, nuclear arms were developed as sophisticated weaponry to suppress violence and uphold peace, but the far-reaching effects of such massive threat to human life necessitated many treaties to limit production and use.

Peace is a work in progress; it is not a utopic idea or an absence of dysfunction. Human weakness and ordinary entropy are part of the natural world and thus, a daily effort is needed to bring about a more unified and harmonious strategy to achieve social justice aimed at preserving the dignity of human life, as well as respecting the living creatures with whom we share the planet by protecting the earth's resources and redirecting our thought processes toward choosing life.

Life-Giving Behaviors and Choices

At the root of many life-giving decisions and choices is the crucial foundation of trust. This essential type of reliance is necessary for us to progress in any given situation. Without trust, relationships fail, governments decay, legal systems crash, business ventures fold and civilizations break down. Trust is a good that sustains all the components of life, growth, and recovery. As humans, we often make mistakes, and we find that rebuilding trust is a difficult, if, sometimes impossible task, so working toward maintaining trust is a key element in life-giving choices and behaviors. Putting all of these tools to work begins by implementing the Choose Life motto in all our behaviors and choices.

Charity and Kindness – create opportunities to bring joy and comfort to others. Treating someone kindly restores hope and multiplies goodness. The opposite of hope is despair, a life-threatening attitude that leads to cynicism and bitterness. Kindness requires that we wish to effect a change wherever we see sorrow, need, and hopelessness. It brings with it the full responsibility of charity, to make the leap into goodness even at the risk of rejection, and to treat others as we wish to be treated. *Random Acts of Kindness* is a philosophy worth revisiting:

> "It all started in a Sausalito, California, restaurant in 1982 when Anne Herbert scrawled the words "practice random acts of kindness and senseless acts of beauty" on a place mat. From there it spread to bumper stickers, quietly at first, but with all the powerful momentum of something important–calling us to lives of caring and compassion. *Random Acts of Kindness*, true stories of acts of kindness, was published in February 1993 and set off a chain reaction. Articles appeared in nearly every newspaper in the U.S., and hundreds of radio stations devoted airtime to the cause. Toward the end of 1993, a Bakersfield, California, professor gave a class assignment to do a random act of kindness–unleashing yet another flood of stories. The concept continues to spread, and we hope it will carry on until the beauty of simple kindness touches–and changes–us all" (According to www.auscharity.org)

For several years, some teachers worked this benevolent concept of random acts of kindness into their curriculum and children were encouraged to perform random, unsolicited acts of pure kindness where, intuitively they identified a need. Older children could be seen shoveling driveways for elderly neighbors while smaller children were encouraged to help a crying peer out of an emotional predicament. But children aren't the only ones that can and should be encouraged to perform acts of kindness – adults should work to set the example. In other words, the only way this practice can truly become a way of life is if it isn't restricted to childhood projects without adult examples and follow-through. It's time once again to take up the banner and move it forward – all acts of kindness, random or otherwise, are life-giving habits.

The benefits of kindness include: improved relationships, individual fulfillment, the power to dismantle unkindness, a better sense of self-worth that leads to well-being and provides a further impetus to spread more kindness. Kindness and charity are life-giving forces that progress in a positive direction, whereas unkindness is a veritable landslide of destruction. One of the most important facets of kindness is the ability to show it when it is most difficult. While it is much easier to demonstrate kindness under pleasurable circumstances, it is a challenge to show kindness in the face of adversity. Don't wait for someone to be kind, show them how it's done. Leo Buscaglia, author and professor of Special Education once wrote, " Too often we underestimate the power of a touch, a smile, a kind word, a listening ear, an honest compliment, or the smallest act of caring, all of which have the potential to turn a life around." We can turn a life around in a positive direction by showing compassion, not only to people we know but also to those we encounter briefly. The caring spirit of charity and kindness has the power to bring something wonderful to life by making room in one's heart for another person.

Imagine walking outside your home each morning and all that could be seen as far as the horizon was mountains of trash, waste, and sewage! Unkindness can leave a visible imprint on the world as hideous as decomposition and decay. Planting the kindest part of oneself into the world can grow and develop into a generative and perpetuating energy. Charity and kindness require attention; this attention can be most fruitful when applied to those who need it most – those who may be difficult to love. Loneliness and despair can be a depreciative force. Encouraging the value of life requires *showing an interest*: to the aged as well as small children, to the poor and sick, to the homeless and neglected, to the disabled and distraught, and to the many who suffer from some type of disorder that inhibits their ability to "blend in."

The Dalai Lama once said, "If you want others to be happy, practice compassion. If you want to be happy, practice compassion."

The dividend of kindness and charity is hope. We have all, at one time or another, experienced both hope and despair. Hope comes from the feeling that we're not alone, that life-giving options are available, that support exists, that powerful influences won't guide us to make decisions that cause us some type of harm that loss is an avenue to new beginnings that life is worth living no matter what happens. Hope, which results from kindness, compassion and genuine caring, is as revitalizing as finding a waterfall of cool spring water in the middle of a desert, and everyone can appreciate it! Mark Twain once said that "Kindness is a language that the deaf can hear and the blind can see." One might add that even those not well-versed in kindness can still experience its effects. Kindness is a language in which we can all become fluent.

Respect – restores dignity which counteracts the effects of humiliation. Dignity doesn't mean that we hide from our mistakes by making excuses, placing blame, or justifying our actions. Treating ourselves and others with respect and dignity means that we acknowledge and take responsibility for our behavior and contemplate how we can grow from our mistakes to go on to living better and healthier lives. Dignity means we must move on from guilt, using it only as a tool to feel adequate remorse for our actions and thus making amends. Acknowledging our self-worth helps us to recognize the value of others and to treat them with dignity as well. Mutual respect, by definition, is a reciprocal, life-giving force that cultivates true progress in our relationships with one another and with the world around us.

Robin S. Dillon, Associate Professor of Philosophy at Lehigh University and editor of *Dignity, Character, and Self-Respect*, has written at great length about the moral significance of self-respect with a regard for its impact on society. She writes,

> "We may also learn that how our lives go depends every bit as much on whether we respect ourselves… Some people find that finally being able to respect themselves is what matters most about getting off welfare, kicking

> a disgusting habit, or defending something they value; others, sadly, discover that life is no longer worth living if self-respect is irretrievably lost. It is part of everyday wisdom that respect and self-respect are deeply connected, that it is difficult if not impossible both to respect others if we don't respect ourselves and to respect ourselves if others don't respect us. It is increasingly part of political wisdom both that unjust social institutions can devastatingly damage self-respect and that robust and resilient self-respect can be a potent force in struggles against injustice."

Respect is a welcoming and revitalizing force – it allows for damaged human dignity, neglected and abused people and other living things, or mistreated earth's resources to be once again healed and restored. If we don't respect the value of human life, if we abuse and mistreat animals, and consume all resources without regard for tomorrow what can our descendants *hope* to inherit from us but a severely damaged and non-productive world?

In Stanford University's *Encyclopedia of Philosophy*, Fall, 2010 edition, Professor Dillon compares the varying aspects of Immanuel Kant's view of respect (18th c.) to that of John Rawls (20th c.):

> "In *The Metaphysics of Morals* (1797), Kant argues for specific duties to oneself generated by the general duty to respect humanity in our persons, including duties to not engage in suicide, misuse of our sexual powers, drunkenness and other unrestrained indulgence of inclination, lying, self-deception, avarice, and servility. Kant also maintains that the duty of self-respect is the most important moral duty, for unless there were duties to respect oneself, there could be no moral duties at all. Moreover, fulfilling our duty to respect ourselves is a necessary condition of fulfilling our duties to respect other persons."

Rawls' views, Dillon points out, regards

> "self-respect neither as something we are morally required to have and maintain nor as a feeling we necessarily have, but as an entitlement that social institutions are required by justice to support and not undermine. In *A Theory of Justice* (1971) he argues that self-respect is a 'primary good,' something that rational beings want whatever else they want, because it is vital to the experienced quality of individual lives and to the ability to carry out or achieve whatever projects or aims an individual might have. It is, moreover, a social good, one that individuals are able to acquire only under certain social and political conditions." Rawls defines self-respect as including "a person's sense of his own value, his secure conviction that his conception of the good, his plan of life, is worth carrying out," and it implies "a confidence in one's ability, so far as it is within one's power, to fulfill one's intentions"

> He argues that individuals' access to self-respect is to a large degree a function of how the basic institutional structure of a society defines and distributes the social bases of self-respect, which include the messages about the relative worth of citizens that are conveyed in the structure and functioning of institutions, the distribution of fundamental political rights and civil liberties, access to the resources individuals need to pursue their plans of life, the availability of diverse associations and communities within which individuals can seek affirmation of their worth and their plans of life from others, and the norms governing public interaction among citizens. Since self-respect is vital to individual well-being, Rawls argues that justice requires that social institutions and policies be designed to support and not

> undermine self-respect. Rawls argues that the principles of justice as fairness are superior to utilitarian principles insofar as they better affirm and promote self-respect for all citizens" (Rawls 1971, 440).

Consideration for both the individual and the social aspects of respect, as seen through the choose life paradigm, requires an attunement of our thought processes toward life as a basis for self-respecting and socially respecting decision-making. If an individual strives to make life choices, the optimal choices would involve those which cause the least amount of harm. For example, I'm not going to drink and drive, not only because it's against the law, but because 1) I have enough self-respect to protect myself from harm and 2) I have enough respect for others to safeguard their right to safety and freedom from potential injury or death. Life decisions factor respect into the equation; respect recognizes that life comes first.

Integrity is born out of self-respect, doing the right thing for the right reason, or as C.S. Lewis put it, "Integrity is doing the right thing, even when no one is watching." Choosing to do the right thing when it is difficult prunes away our weaknesses and allows room for growth and strengthening of character. Integrity requires honesty when deception would make the situation easier. It also necessitates a firm loyalty to uphold moral and ethical laws because of a high regard for oneself. Integrity is like a preservative for a quality life and for all things which are good and worth keeping. Deceitfulness, cheating, and manipulation are forces that oppose integrity and only serve to destroy our inner good, the good in others, and the good in our relationships. If integrity is sacrificed in decision-making, the consequences have ample repercussions, not only will character suffer, but family members, friends, colleagues, neighbors and the community will eventually be impacted. Everyone is familiar with this corollary; the "black sheep" whose life impacts the family directly or indirectly, the unreliable friend, the co-worker whose behavior is erratic, the neighbors that seem to weaken the stability of the neighborhood.

Life is work. It takes a concerted effort each day to rise and live up to our highest potential. As the old proverb reminds us, "A job worth doing is worth doing well." Life is a job worth doing well – when we witness someone living life to the fullest, it looks like art. Directing our best energy into the work we do, the relationships we have, and the joys we share may bring about an invigorating attitude with infectious outcomes. Just as negativity can foster low morale and depressing environments; integrity fueled by life-affirming choices creates an atmosphere of wholesomeness. *Live today well*, a motivational motto pronounced by the Salesians, an affirmative and upbeat religious order whose work in charity is well-known, is a principle rooted in the beauty of the human person, our potential *to be who we are and be that well.*

Behaviors that encourage integrity are anchored in accepted human values. Many businesses have adopted workplace standards to promote a healthy work environment for it is known that an atmosphere that lacks integrity soon shows a decline in business, a high turnover in employees, and a diminished capacity for customer service and relations – the beginning of the end of the business. Business standards recommend:

> "*Golden Rule* - Treating others the way you want to be treated is the core principle of the golden rule and an example of how workers can display integrity in the workplace. Practicing the golden rule ensures that disturbances that may distract or offend others remain at bay while in a work setting. The golden rule is a reflection of respect for others.
>
> *Honesty* - honesty is an optimal example of integrity in the workplace. Honesty encourages open communication between employers, employees and co-workers. It leads to effective relationships in an organization. When workers are honest about the various aspects of their jobs that need improvement, employers can take action and help. Employers that are open about company

> policies and changes that affect the organization are more trustworthy from the employees' perspective.
>
> *Confidentiality* - Confidentiality is a prime example of integrity in the workplace. It is also a legal necessity. Employers have an obligation to keep certain information private. Violation of privacy policies could lead to fines, penalties and possible lawsuits. Confidentiality instills trust and encourages sincere consideration of the privacy of others.
>
> *Lead by Example* - Employers and employees can display integrity in the workplace through leading by example. When individuals lead by example, they set the foundation for appropriate workplace behavior. Leading by example improves personal awareness, sensitivity to others and accountability which are all necessary for ethical behavior and integrity" (Sherrie Scott).

As we can see, some of these foundation principles begin to repeat throughout the various areas where we strive for a life-giving approach to sustain healthy living. These same principles apply to our relationships with family and friends as well, where strife may be common because of the habitual way we treat each other. Integrity in relationships cannot rule out any of the above foundation principles. For bonds to grow between people it is necessary to treat others with kindness and respect and to keep the lines of communication open. There are many way we can break down those lines of communication by undermining trust. Some people invite confidence by explaining that they are not judgmental and then turn around and make the person feel as if they have been criticized or invalidated through a tell-tale silence which leaves them with a feeling of humiliation. This deflating habit exploits human dignity, leaving the disheartened person feeling like they've just removed all their clothes and are now being ridiculed for being naked. The same is true for confidentiality – once a person has revealed an important confidence, it is vital to respect the life of an act of trust by treating the gift with discretion. Erica Jong, author, teacher and poet, once said, "Gossip is the opiate of oppression." Repeating confidences suppresses growth and damages trust – trust is the soil in which life-giving opportunities are allowed to grow freely.

Leading by example, a necessary element of integrity in a growing environment, is found at every level of the human social stratum: in political leadership, education, business, law, community and family. Integrity and trust work hand-in-hand and demand responsibility – the responsibility to establish a method of living for those around us and in our care, as well as for generations to come. By establishing good examples and traditions based on integrity and life-affirming decisions, we set the ball in motion that can benefit our lives and humanity.

Honesty is a kindness, it is respectful and it coincides with integrity. Honesty is the sunlight which illuminates who we truly are. It also allows for that light to strengthen us, to see the areas where we need improvement and to reach for the serenity that comes from accepting the things we can change and having the courage to change the things we can. For personal growth to occur, honesty, genuineness, and a commitment to natural humanness helps to develop the spirit of life-affirming choices. There is harmony when our values are honestly reflected by the choices we make. Being honest with ourselves is as important as being honest with others. If we delude ourselves, it's impossible to be truly honest with others.

Honesty should never be used as a weapon to hurt another – once that line has been crossed it is no longer a life-giving choice but can be destructive in nature. As poet, Don Marquis once wrote,

> "honesty is a good
> thing but
> it is not profitable to
> its possessor
> unless it is kept under control" (archygrams, archy's life of mehitabel).

Honesty can be a nurturing attribute to strengthen character as well as the soul, just as vitamins are needed to nourish the body. Honesty in healthy doses is beneficial while brutal honesty can damage self-worth, just as mega doses of certain vitamins can become toxic. Learning to moderate the goods of nature is an essential lesson. In practicing moderation, we leave room for growth in ourselves and for the benefit of those around us. One can infuse goodness into a relationship by the use of honesty or destroy it completely by abusing the gift that ultimately hurts another. At one time or another we may have experienced the thrashing effects of honesty spoken with malice. The key to life-affirming honesty is to apply it gently and with kindness. Harshness leads to denial anyway; it spurns growth and may cut off future opportunities by damaging trust.

As with any "good," honesty can be subject to these types of misuse, and therein lies a new choice: to use the truth for good, or to manipulate the truth to one's advantage. Quite often, people distort the truth with a process of rationalization. This type of "truth-telling" cuts up the real truth into little pieces and reassembles them (perhaps leaving part of them out) into a new version of the "truth." The message may ring true because it contains elements of the truth but it is far from representing the whole reality. Truth manipulation is not honesty. Sometimes, people are so desperate to hear what they need to hear, that they are willing to forget that.

There is a self-preservation aspect to honesty as well. The lessons in honesty begin from the first moments we achieve enough autonomy to make our own decisions. Once a mistake is made and someone attempts to hold us accountable, we have the choice to be honest, which may result in a negative consequence, or to be dishonest as a means to safeguard our choice, which, as we've often seen, results in a ripple-effect of problems. Mistakes have their own innate consequences; dishonesty has the potential to destroy something that is very difficult to regain: respect. Being known as a liar is damaging to our self-respect, our integrity, and our character. We learn about what we can get away with from an early age. *As long as I don't get caught* or *I didn't do anything wrong* are among the most self-deceptive mistakes we can make. This type of thinking shifts the focus from the value of *honesty* to the problem of *getting caught*, so that if there are no consequences for dishonesty unless it is exposed, then it is not a wrongful action. We begin to learn this valuable lesson at home with our parents, caregivers, siblings, and peers, but it most dramatically felt in the arena of the school environment. Many school systems, teachers, and universities struggle with the problem of academic honesty, one of the fundamental areas geared toward the character-building aspects of education.

> "Academic honesty is very important for students because the well being of the student community regarding their performance in academics depends on this particular factor. When one student cheats and gets a better grade, then he or she is cheating every other student who is really working hard to find their way to better grades" (homemorals.com).

Once again, we are confronted with the ramifications of personal choice. Academic honesty does not impact the individual student alone; it affects the entire educational community by devaluing the worth of the learning process. Some schools, in an attempt to address this issue, have resorted to removing an academic penalty for cheating by addressing the issue as a behavioral, rather than an academic problem. The student does not receive a failing grade for cheating, but must redo the work for a grade. When polled, college students expressed a general consensus that if they knew they wouldn't receive an "F" for cheating, they would simply learn how to cheat in a more successful way. They felt that, though an "F" does not always deter cheating, it goes a long way to reminding one of the consequences.

> "Academics put the student's abilities and capabilities to test. If a student gets away by cheating, then their true worth can never be proven. Also, such students may get by at their college level and enjoy the false pride about their grades. However, when it comes to finding employment, they really have to prove what they have done and also show their achievements through their skills. Cheating, plagiarism, deception and fabrication of facts are all types of academic dishonesty. In the

> United States, statistics show that nearly 70 percent of the students are involved in academic dishonesty. Students resort to all kinds of dishonest means when they see the result being positive, and the rate of it only increasing as time goes by" (homemorals.com).

While academic penalties have not been entirely successful in solving the problem of dishonesty, the drawback of removing an academic penalty when students cheat is that it reflects the mouse-in-the maze model: if my goal is to get an "A" through cheating, I simply have to find a better way to do so. Educators run the risk of developing a better population of cheaters. This philosophy does not sit well with the real world. When students reach the workplace, they bring the character of dishonesty with them. If it served them well in school, it cannot hurt to try it at work. Imagine employers asking an embezzler to redo the books without misappropriating funds this time and allowing them to keep their jobs! Embezzlement, abuses, bribes, stealing, fraud, lying, privacy breaches, cheating all constitute white collar crimes that incur serious penalties, including the loss of work and respect, and possibility of accountability for criminal charges. Dishonesty takes something valuable away from any environment, whether it is school, the workplace, a family or a community. As a result of dishonesty, the social and organizational environment suffers and becomes depleted of the necessary life-giving atmosphere where people and their efforts are safe to grow and develop.

The attributes of honesty, as with many of the tools being discussed, are highly dependent on an understanding of ethics. The Ethics Resource Center (ERC) conducted an important survey in 2010 to study *The Importance of Ethical Culture.* In order to create stronger ethical business practices, the report found that it is necessary to create an "ethical culture" where employers and employees adhere to morals and principles founded in rudimentary ethics. The ERC reports that,

> "In a 'strong' ethical culture, ethical values matter and that is apparent in the actions of employees (especially

> management), company policies and procedures, and decisions about who gets rewarded, who gets punished, and how to weather the tough times. In a 'weak' ethical culture, values are not promoted and 'getting the job done' is far more important than getting the job done in an ethically *right* way. Basically, the company's ethical culture is the extent to which the organization makes doing the right thing a priority" (ethics.org).

Businesses, educational institutions, legal systems, political arenas, medical communities, and families all share the responsibility of developing an ethical culture. It cannot succeed unless everyone works together consistently. These various institutions overlap and if ethical standards fail in one area, it weakens the entire structure. We need to work together to put all our ethical ideas and goals on the same page. Honesty and honor, respect and integrity are crucial to the advancement of an ethical culture. Ethics promote a living structure; ethics endorse life; and by compartmentalizing ethics to mean different things in different arenas, we find that values such as honesty are compromised. Whenever we tolerate a certain amount of dishonesty in any domain we must struggle even harder to attain an ethical and life-giving culture.

Gratitude is an essential ingredient to the life-giving aspects of our humanness. Gratitude has a way of multiplying what is indispensably good and creates new avenues of opportunities for generosity. Without gratitude, the life-giving effects of kindness can be destroyed. How many times have we encountered someone who is hurt by ingratitude? Certainly, our kindness should never be extended with the expectation of gratitude, but appreciation is a life-force that builds on kindness. Gratitude is a self-perpetuating spirit that moves forward and opens doors to more life-giving behaviors, while ingratitude may very well slam those doors shut! Gratitude gives life to the greater good. The feeling of wanting to "give back" for all the blessings one has received advances the work of kindness.

Rabbi Abraham Joshua Heschel wrote in *Who is Man?* that,

> "There is a built-in sense of indebtedness in the consciousness of man, an awareness of owing gratitude, of being called upon at certain moments to reciprocate, to answer, to live in a way which is compatible with the grandeur and mystery of living."

Gratitude allows us to participate in the expansion of goodness. Showing gratitude for a kindness is conventional – we receive a birthday gift, a helping hand, helpful advice, a joyful experience and we find ways to say thank you, in words, a note, or a gesture of goodwill in return. What is profoundly unconventional is trying to discover the opportunity for gratitude when it is difficult and we are challenged to grow. There are times when we become complacent with standard forms of generosity and we fall short of placing value on gratitude. Situations where someone is offering help, advice, wisdom, or even discipline where none has been requested are often met with ingratitude. Parents, teachers, managers among others often encounter unappreciative responses to these situations. If a mentor has imposed an uncomfortable challenge that requires more effort than one is willing to perform, gratitude may not be forthcoming. A mature realization that growth may often involve some effort and perhaps even some discomfort allows a person to meet the challenge with an attitude of gratitude.

Author William Arthur Ward once wrote that "Feeling gratitude and not expressing it is like wrapping a present and not giving it." We can develop a grateful mindset by continually seeing the lessons in life as gifts that may sometimes hurt but challenge us to grow. Gratitude expressed only for the "feel-good" situations in life can seriously limit our ability to be grateful. We can learn to be grateful for times when someone must point out our shortcomings, moments when we failed to show consideration for others, or times when we've been held accountable for mistakes. Malicious reprisals for these situations can escalate into a detrimental scenario, but a modest acknowledgement of our slip-ups can reduce negativity and expand the opportunity for constructive relations. Gratitude has been studied in areas other than social as well.

> "Stress from the daily flux of good and bad in our lives can produce anxiety, tension, anger and pain in our lives. These negative emotions can lead to physical pain as tense muscles, higher blood pressure and unhealthy coping mechanisms combine to bring you down an undesirable path. One way to combat negativity and stress is to practice gratitude, focusing your mind and energy on the positive in your life. The benefits of expressing gratitude have even been documented in scientific studies. It appears that expressing gratitude works as a protective, healing, emotional energy force" (Rachel Mork, Life123.com).

Practices which promote healing are considered to be life-affirming and beneficial. It's important to take time each day to remember the things for which we are grateful, and to find a way to express it. Gratitude increases an atmosphere of thoughtfulness, thoughts which lead to life-producing actions.

Patience and gentleness – These are powerful tools in the growing process. Have you ever tried to grow flowers from seed? Impatience has no place in growth. There are many actions you can take (such as over-watering, exposing the plants to more sunlight, or prodding the soil) to hurry the process of growth along but these measures won't speed up the growth process and may likely put an end to it. Gentleness stems from an understanding that life is precious and should be treated delicately. Parents and teachers understand that patience and gentleness is required on a daily basis. Without these life-affirming efforts, children cannot grow up properly, particularly if the environment is harsh, abusive, or hurtful. But patience and gentleness should not be construed as an absence of self-discipline, nor does it mean that we should patiently tolerate injustices to human dignity. Guidance and correction are actions that can be exercised along with diligence and patience. It has often been evident that patience is what is required after you've used up all that you thought was patience.

Patience and gentleness go hand-in-hand with courtesy and politeness. Etiquette guru, Emily Post, wrote extensively on appropriate human conduct and manners and what she termed the Best Society.

> "Etiquette must, if it is to be of more than trifling use, include ethics as well as manners. Certainly what one is, is of far greater importance than what one appears to be. A knowledge of etiquette is of course essential to one's decent behavior... Thus Best Society is not a fellowship of the wealthy, nor does it seek to exclude those who are not of exalted birth; but it is an association of gentle-folk, of which good form in speech, charm of manner, knowledge of the social amenities, and instinctive consideration for the feelings of others, are the credentials by which society the world over recognizes its chosen members" (bartleby.com).

Patience and gentleness are called into action in tense, unstable, or perilous situations not when everything is at peace. Patience is an individual as well as a social attitude. Rules of etiquette, manners, and civility have been transformed into an ideology of political correctness, and while it's useful to clean up language, PC does not take the place of common courtesy. It is quite beneficial to eliminate insensitive verbiage but the shortfall of modern political correctness is that it has no cohesion or organized standard between good deeds and behavior. It contains an element of inconsistency. A professional who uses all the correct phraseology in an office environment may drive aggressively, unsafely, and extend any number of gestures to fellow drivers on the commute home. In order to integrate patience, gentleness, manners, courtesy and civility into life patterns, these modes of behavior must become a consistent habit in our encounters with other people. This is why, perhaps, political correctness has not adequately replaced the broader concept of civility. If its implications extend only to linguistics in a professional environment, schools, or the media, but fails to reach the governance of conduct in all settings, then it's just *words*.

Good behavior requires more effort than rhetoric. Patience is a beautiful word, and rudeness sounds as ugly as it is, but transforming our life choices into a more positive growth pattern necessitates that we begin to connect a lot of dots between beauty and action; and malice and reaction. Words have very little meaning without actions to support them. We can demonstrate patience by widening the scope of our willingness to be kind and generous; this often means that we must show kindness and generosity to those we feel may not deserve it. Returning rudeness-for-rudeness is a damaging pattern, while responding to discourteous behavior with patience and gentleness can weaken a destructive pattern. Life-giving choices redirect our behaviors and decisions to those actions which give birth to goodness rather than ruthlessness, annoyance, intolerance, and violence. Choosing life means having the patience to watch things grow, to treat things with a gentle touch especially if they're bruised, neglected, or damaged by the carelessness of the world. We can apply patience and gentleness to relationships, communities, and society; we can correct and prune away the harmfulness of hatred and anger of the over-stressed and overburdened members of our communities; we can stop turning a blind eye to inconsistent social ills, hoping that the right government official will take care of the problems. Social neglect doesn't bear fruitfulness. We need to tend to the world around us. Children's author Frances Hodgson Burnett wrote a charming novel in 1911 about an orphaned British girl living in India, neglected by her parents, and who, after their death, is sent to live with unknown relatives in England. Her uncle is a lonely and depressed man who has nothing more to offer her than an expansive home and food to eat. The child, Mary Lennox, discovers a cousin kept in concealment, and a secret garden, disabused and long forgotten. She makes it her mission to undo the patterns of misguided care to her cousin and to care and nurture the garden and finally brings not only the garden, but the entire household, back to life by the end of the story. "If you look the right way, you can see that the whole world is a garden" (Burnett). It is a worthwhile effort to adjust our view and see the world as a garden which can be tended, nurtured and brought to life.

Creativity, as a work-in-action, has long-been thought to belong to artistic territory. A person is considered creative if they have some form of artsy talent – painting, sculpting, making jewelry or any number of eye-catching crafts – its meaning also covers a wider gamut of poets, authors, musicians, etc… In truth, creativity has spread to realms never before imagined – technology and business implement creativity to find innovative and original ways to develop and market products. Creativity is a momentum that gives life to something new, born from the desire to invent or improve on an idea. The whole philosophy behind creativity is to introduce something new and wonderful to the world and share it with others. Like anything else, creativity may be misused and creations may ironically be destructive, but in the true life-force of creativity, progress is the goal.

Creativity often involves original thinking or, at the very least, the willingness to try something that has not been tried before. When we employ creativity in our relationships, work habits, and daily tasks, the aim is to bring new life and new energy to our endeavors. Treating ourselves, our relationships with others, or even our relationship with God in a creative way can infuse new life into the relationship and help us discover new possibilities. A new perspective can create a feeling of joy. The creative spirit may open doors to new possibilities, strengthen relationships and generate growth. Suddenly, one feels that they have embarked on a new path, and broken away from a feeling of stagnation. There is a profound energy to be discovered when one experiences something new. As Frances Hodgson Burnett wrote, "At first people refuse to believe that a strange new thing can be done, then they begin to hope it can be done, then they see it can be done--then it is done and all the world wonders why it was not done centuries ago" (*The Secret Garden*). This statement echoes the words of 13th century friar, St. Francis of Assisi, who is credited for having said, "Start by doing what's necessary; then do what's possible; and suddenly you are doing the impossible." Creativity doesn't always begin with a magical spark; sometimes it involves a simple dedication to persevere through difficulties, in order to discover what lies ahead. Creativity begins with a commitment to life, to things that grow, and to revitalization.

Thinking of creativity only as a gift places restrictions on its infinite possibilities; creativity is a choice – a choice to open a treasure trove of opportunities, to be open to life's options, to accept something for ourselves and to bring something to others, to our work, and to the world. Creativity is a life-choice when it is open to goodness and not destructiveness. We find that creativity is most fruitful when it is allowed to thrive in morality, honesty and integrity, kindness and charity, respect and gratitude. It cannot flourish in a malicious or crushing atmosphere. It blossoms in intrinsic goodness. Creativity is a life-choice because it creates new choices, those choices that invite promise – it is a powerful tool to supply life with more life by not bringing an end to something good. The value of creativity is in its inherent quality to receive and bring forth. One is open to accept its inspiration and to share the benefits of that inspiration.

Creativity should never be mistaken for a conniving or manipulative force that seeks to ruin something good or to destroy possibilities. Creativity is an energy that perseveres in bringing humanity to its highest potential, not to reduce it to stagnation or limited productivity. Once a person arrives at a point when they feel like they can do no better, one generally closes the door to creativity. When a choice is made that denies life-affirming opportunities, the results then become not creative, but final, and extinguish the prospect of alternatives. A serious problem that seeks a creative solution benefits from the trove of opportunities that life has to offer. Author Eric Hoffer in *The Ordeal of Change* wrote,

> "Discontent is at the root of the creative process… the most gifted members of the human species are at their creative best when they cannot have their way, and must compensate for what they miss by realizing and cultivating their capacities and talents."

It is true that the challenges presented by dissatisfaction with one's circumstances can lead to the discovery of new options but this process is not limited to "the most gifted members of the human species."

Within each of us lies the necessary ingredient to generate change. We all have the power to create, to improve upon ourselves, and to progress. Composer Igor Stravinsky once said that "In order to create there must be a dynamic force, and what force is more potent than love?" The very foundation for all that can grow and develop is love. Surely, Stravinsky could not have composed such masterpieces as *The Nightingale, The Rite of Spring* or *The Firebird* without love. He firmly believed that "Music praises God." God, the creator, the instiller of love planted within each human being the power to love and to create. This boundless love and creative energy is most audible in musical works of art, most perceptible in the visual arts, or most tangible in nature and its bounty. Love illuminates the creative spirit. Without love, choices can be made in darkness and despair, not allowing for the broader vision of future choices.

With a firm understanding that creativity and love exist in the world because God, the creator, instilled it within his living creation, one can become an integral part of the loving and creative process. John Micheal Talbot, Franciscan author and musician, in his book *Blessings*, draws on the writings of Thomas à Kempis and Bonaventure when he explains the evidentiary nature of God's presence in creation,

> "Seeing God does begin here on earth by looking through the glass of creation... Bonaventure says that all creation bears the traces of God. In a very real sense, the pure of heart are able to see God through God's traces in creation."

This type of purity, as explained by Talbot, encompasses all of the synonyms for goodness contained herein: from decency and honor to integrity and honesty. Openness to creativity recognizes that we are a part of creation and we can fulfill the living spirit within us by becoming a bigger part of it. Reticence rejects the opportunities to be creative in favor of rationales or reason. We make excuses for not finding or looking for creative options. An artificial sense of creativity employs selectivity and compartmentalization by being open to life and goodness in one arena while rejecting it in another. At times we apply a double-standard which allows for selective growth, where a destructive idea or thought is nurtured, and a life-giving inspiration is dismissed. Sincerity gives us an advantage over this type of insular thinking that serves as a pitfall to good intentions. Refocusing the decision-making process by using a consistent life-affirming standard helps us to recognize the advantages of having an abundance of alternatives.

As instruments of peace and goodwill, we each carry the responsibility to take care of one another, to support each other, and to work together. By becoming a small prototype of what we would like for all of society to be, we can individually carry the gifts we would like to bequeath and those we would like to receive. Each person can become a storage pantry of gifts, talents, and abilities that we can readily contribute to the world by making choices that benefit the life of all, and setting an example of how this can be accomplished.

Life thoughts

When we have the right to do something but the action itself isn't right, we must employ some key virtues into the decision to act. Happiness is achieved by distinguishing between what we have a right to do, and what is morally right and acting in a way that promotes the general welfare of humanity. On our journey through life we carry with us a very valuable collection of tools that can make the journey more pleasant for us as well as for others. The more often we use these life-giving tools, the more happy and meaningful the journey.

A Wellspring for the Living

Sometimes choosing life can use some help. There is no question about it, making a life-choice may be the more difficult choice to make and it might even feel impossible without support. In order for people to benefit from choices that promote life and for society to profit from an abundance of life-giving choices, a network of "life-support" is required. If society persists in a tug-of-war between individual moral relativism and a moral ideology that lacks supportive action it will be very difficult to create a more consistent pattern of life for all humanity.

Becoming a resource of things that people need

One can stock up on positive attributes and resources to be of help to others that may be running low and faced with difficult choices. It is a logical assumption that if each person is well-stocked with life-giving tools, talents, traits, gifts, and goods and are readily available to help those in need, eventually the overall need subsides as we all become more life-affirming. Things to keep in the storage units of our hearts include, but are not limited to:

Being a good listener – set yourself aside, and open your ears and hearts to those that may simply need the kindness of attention and the ability to vent. Many poor decisions are made without sounding them out in an objective atmosphere. Modern society has no shortage of communication avenues between the variety of phones, computers, devices and apps, and networking systems. We can find resources, but those resources must be willing to lend an ear.

Take time to tune in to the world. When people become parents, suddenly they are tuned into a cacophony of new sounds and become adapted to listening unconsciously for the sounds of a baby stirring in the middle of the night or a scuffle between two children trying to possess the same toy. They have adapted their hearing to interpreting messages: the sound of running water when a toddler has gotten into the bathroom may indicate potential problems, the sound of doors or windows opening at three in the morning when teenagers are about may warn of impending mischief, or the absolute sound of silence when there are five children in the next room could spell trouble. Being an attuned listener means not just hearing what someone is trying to tell us directly, but also listening for the subtler messages that convey a sense of need. What do our young people need if they are writing songs about violence? Whose voices are being suppressed while the louder proclamations of hedonism are trying to distract us? Are the popular messages drowning out the sounds of the important ones?

Listen more attentively – because sometimes there are things that need to be said. The information age in which we find ourselves bombards us with messages from every corner of the world; listening to the messages we *need* to hear may present us with an impossible task. How large is our internet message system? "Eric Schmidt, the CEO of Google, the world's largest index of the Internet, estimated the size at roughly 5 million terabytes of data. That's over 5 billion gigabytes of data, or 5 trillion megabytes" (wisegeek.com). This phenomenon would be like two parents trying to listen to countless children all at the same time, or one teacher trying to discern the messages of students everywhere all at once, or a dispatch officer trying to respond to emergency calls following a widespread natural disaster. It is quite possible that the seven billion people in the world are struggling to send the same message in millions of different ways: that we need to make loving choices; we need to make *life* choices; we need to support one another and care for each other. Listening is much like generosity, we can't obtain more of what we need by hoarding the sound waves; we receive more input by sharing what we have with others – the ability to *listen*.

Prayer – never underestimate the value of stocking your life with prayer. There is always need for prayer and the gift can be so freely given on the spot. Toni Brasted, Ph.D., writing for Compassioncarehospice.com, reminds us that affiliation to a particular religion does not matter, prayer has tremendous benefits:

> "Prayers are our opportunity to speak with God... Prayer is the state of being where we invite in all of heaven to support, nurture, and guide our lives... Prayer is an attitude of Gratitude where we remind ourselves we are not alone, that there is a Presence surrounding us that is far greater than any difficulty we face. Prayer allows for the energy of healing. When we pray, the floodgates are open to wash away any fear or doubt... A prayer is the asking of our heart; connecting with its Home. Ultimately, prayer is the opportunity for God to express through us, renewing our Faith, renewing our Trust, and renewing our strength in the oneness of all things. A prayer is our wake-up call to once again invite God into our lives. A prayer can be a powerful healing tool."

Prayer can be offered at various intervals throughout the day. Members of the Islamic faith pray five times a day; those of the Jewish faith offer devotional prayers throughout course of the day in the morning, midday and in the evening. Christians, practicing the prayer life of the Liturgy of the Hours keep prayer at the forefront of their daily lives by joining their prayers with those of the whole church by "praying continually." Formal prayer is not the only method of praying; stopping to connect with God, the source of life is a way to remain connected with the strength that we need when faced with difficult life choices. God is always there. Prayer is always available to us. Some choose to keep a notebook or prayer journal at all times so that when the need for prayer arises, or someone asks for prayers it is easy to jot it down and take a moment to give life to our thoughts and intentions.

Generosity – our participation in good works has unlimited value. It's an extension of kindness when we help others in need. When we work together the benefits are increased exponentially. In a broadcast, Archbishop Fulton Sheen once said,

> "True generosity never looks to reciprocity; it gives neither because it expects a gift in return, nor because there is a duty or obligation to give. Charity lies beyond obligation, its essence is the 'adorable extra'. Its reward is the joy of giving."

The true spirit of generosity begins with the self. We must each be willing to give of ourselves freely and unconditionally. This is a "life-support" choice that benefits each individual and society as a whole. The danger that lies in a utopic idea of generosity from which stem the commonality theories of Socialism, Marxism, Communism, and Distributism is that it diminishes personal responsibility. If one feels absolved of personal duty because of taxes that share the wealth, then one may not feel obliged to give of oneself *personally*. This sentiment was most succinctly articulated by one of Charles Dickens' most memorable character, Ebenezer Scrooge, in *A Christmas Carol*,

> "Are there no prisons?..And the Union Workhouses? Are they still in operation?...The Treadmill and the Poor Law are in full vigour, then? … I'm very glad to hear it… I can't afford to make idle people merry. I help to support the establishments I have mentioned; they cost enough; and those who are badly off must go there."

Once the spirit of generosity is compromised by collective mandates and taxation, it is difficult to realize our full human potential to give as individuals and to receive. C.S. Lewis, in an effort to clarify the benefits of almsgiving wrote,

> "Charity – giving to the poor is an essential part of Christian morality... Some people nowadays say that charity ought to be unnecessary and that instead of giving to the poor we ought to be producing a society in which there are no poor to give to. They may be quite right in saying that we ought to produce that kind of society. But, if anyone thinks that, as a consequence, you can stop giving in the meantime, then he has parted with all Christian morality... For many of us the great obstacle to charity lies not in our own luxurious living or desire for more money, but in our fear – fear of insecurity."

Generosity of spirit is a willingness to give to those who are poor and in need (in the financial sense), but also to those who may have emotional and spiritual needs, as well as the need for familial care and friendship. Generosity is the ability to help someone feel that they are not alone, that someone cares. Generosity is a choice to give someone hope. It works together with hospitality which is a gift that opens the way to friendship, love, compassion, goodwill, sympathy, and consideration. We create room in our lives for other people who may need us.

Stability – when we remain faithful in a difficult situation we foster stability which allows room for growth and improvement. However, this does not mean that we should remain in an abusive or destructive relationship or environment for this situation is not life-giving but tragically detrimental. When the situation is no longer improving but injurious, it is considered unstable and unhealthy. We owe it to ourselves, our families, our friends, neighbors, co-workers and communities to make life-choices that promote stability and to seek help when those choices become difficult. Stability benefits the world by offering steady ground in which life can grow.

Be of good Character – If we could put our character under a microscope we would find that the character cells are comprised of a lifetime of choices. Character is revealed not only through our actions, but most clearly through our *reactions*. Actions are often planned, or may have benefited from a modicum of thought, but reactions tend to expose more about our character because we don't always have the time to think, or perhaps we do think and decide to go with our first impulse. This is one reason why habits are so important – by making conscious decisions to choose life-affirming options on a regular basis, our reactions will soon become ingrained with our actions. Begin by being very mindful of every decision, no matter how minor or how critical - from choosing a healthy cereal to handling a traffic snafu or confronting conflicts in relationships with patience and charity. Use a choose-life blue print for all decisions.

Strengthen your habits with regular character exercise: build a good reputation by being honest and dependable; earn respect rather than expecting it; practice fairness and kindness when it seems most difficult (especially in your *reactions*); persevere at making life-giving choices; show self-control in all choices; practice good manners; remain aware of the effects of your decisions; be genuine.

Community and friendship can be the greatest defense against loneliness and fear. The bonds of friendship and community strengthen the spirit by endowing everyone with a sense of acceptance. What is critical to remember is that for community and friendship to survive acceptance is necessary, however, excusing behavior that is not life-giving will eventually chip away at the foundations of the social infrastructure. Loving, accepting and supporting a friend or member of the community should also come with guidance toward a better understanding of the non-life-giving behavior. If a person is committing some action that hurts himself, society will be affected as well. If there are *many* injured members of society there will be a tremendous need for healing both the individual and the whole – not healing one without the other. By building stronger communities and friendships we can support and heal one another. "Act so as to encourage the best in others, and by doing so you will develop the best in yourself" (Edward Ericson, *The Humanist Way: An Intro to Ethical Humanist Religion*).

Joy and celebration – Much has been written about joy and its importance to our very existence. Humans desire, almost more than anything to be happy, but often find that happiness is temporary, and we search for ways to make it a more stable influence in our lives. The crux of the matter is not only how to achieve happiness, but how to keep it. Joy is a deeper, more stable feeling and it is difficult to contain – it wishes to be exposed, expressed, and multiplied. The most common way to enrich the life of joy is to share it. As St. Augustine once said, "When large number of people share their joy in common, the happiness of each is greater because each adds fuel to the other's flame." Joy reaches its highest potential when it is freely spread to others, it is never meant to be kept to oneself.

As humans we feel tremendous joy when love is present – these two forces are absolutely intertwined. When we give of ourselves out of love, we experience as much joy as when someone shares their gift of love with us. Life provides us with the banquet where love and joy may be most fully expressed. By saying yes to love and life, we are inviting joy into our lives that is meant to be shared with others.

Life offers opportunities for joy but as anyone can confirm, it isn't always easy. Our choices may result in sorrow, or we may encounter new problems to solve. We may be negatively impacted by the choices of others that threaten our happiness. Predicaments that are beyond our control may continually force us to find new ways to heal so that we may once again experience joy. *Alcoholics Anonymous,* a widespread group that supports recovery and aids those suffering from addiction helps its members by steering them away from fear, anxiety, loneliness and self-destructive behaviors by concentrating on the joys of life and celebrating each moment by building a support network. Its principles include honesty and humility, reflection and truth, willingness and commitment, surrender and atonement, vigilance and service, embracing oneness with God and finding hope. These precepts give way to new life and purpose as well as giving each person a reason to find joy in the moment, even through the struggles, and never to forget to celebrate life. These invaluable precepts are worth stocking up on! Making choices that bring joy means saying yes to love and life!

Words – In the words of Buddha (Siddhartha Gautama) "Words have the power to both destroy and heal. When words are both true and kind, they can change our world." The choice to use words to hurt someone or help them is one of the most frequent choices we make. The age-old proverb, *choose your words carefully*, has long-since warned us about the critical nature of self-expression, and how a measure of thoughtfulness can guide our words in a supportive manner. Once again, truth should never be used as a weapon to do harm. Life-affirming words help to maintain relationships, to create a positive morale in the workplace or any environment, or to bring comfort to those who need it. The primary intention of using the language of love and care should be to *do good*. Influential people, however, have at times used life-affirming language to entice people into complying with harmful agendas. Saying what people need to hear must be founded in good intentions and life-affirming choices.

Practice friendly communication – don't just work on being "politically correct" but endeavor to be "socially correct." Kindness, respectfulness, honesty, patience, gentleness, gratefulness all have a place in our daily communications. Never forget to tell someone you care about them. With the unpredictability of life always hanging in the balance, it is important to share words of comfort, support, encouragement, and concern. Telling a stranger to have a nice day extends the idea that one cares. Remember – where words fail – *smile*. Disagreements are often unavoidable, but remember to choose words that at least attempt to communicate care rather than malice – some words cause irreparable damage and bring an end to something that was once good.

Courage – there are times when it takes much more courage to make the life-giving choice than it does to make a choice that results in entropy. "Courage is about the risk that promotes the greater good, which justifies the danger." (Steve Johnson, Director of Character Education, Markkula Center for Applied Ethics). It takes a well-developed sense of courage to behave ethically, morally and socially responsible. When speaking about character education, Johnson goes on to say that,

> "... it's about promoting pro-social thoughts, values, and behaviors and having students act as good citizens should in school. In others, it's about developing specific desirable values.

For schools in general, character education is about finding some way to help students develop good habits or virtues."

Good habits and virtues help us to form the type of character that is required to make life-choices. It is often far easier to cave in to routine decisions that might be self-serving than to face the decision that might cause the least amount of harm to those around us. Get in the habit of using courage as a tool to choose life in any situation. Make your courage available to others so that they may benefit in their struggles. One of the earliest life skills we learn is about standing up to peer pressure. It is very difficult to maintain your sense of values when your friends, and people you admire, are expressing precarious views. In his book, *A Landscape with Dragons*, Michael D. O'Brien illustrates the point that in our contemporary world it may take more courage than ever to retain the core values and virtues that benefit an entire culture. He argues that,

> "We cannot assume that we will be immune to the massive apostasy that is taking place in the Western world. Never in human history has there been such a wholesale loss of faith, nor one that has come about with such startling speed. Much of its momentum is due to the unprecedented power of television, film, and video—of the image—to recreate our understanding of the very shape of reality. Thus, large numbers of Christians simply do not realize that they are apostacizing, and still larger numbers do not understand that they are being prepared mentally to follow. This is the power of impressionism; it is also 'peer pressure' on a colossal scale. How very difficult it is to resist an entire culture, and especially for children to do so, because it is a right and good thing for children to grow into awareness of being members of a broader community. They need culture in order to grow properly. It is one of their

> primary means of learning what it is to be a fully human person in a community of fellow human beings."

Social networking has made it easier for friends and families, colleagues and acquaintances, to be in contact with one another, but the ability to preserve one's values in the face of such widespread exposure has given new meaning to the word *courage*. We are facing peer pressure everywhere we turn. It takes a particular quality of mind and determination to defend life, and the values that promote life if one's views are suddenly, and blaringly different than the philosophy of popular culture. Courage has an *encouraging* value. In the words of evangelist, Billy Graham, "Courage is contagious. When a brave man takes a stand, the spines of others are often stiffened."

Trust –is much like a social glue that holds a society together when both individual and collective choices are made to benefit, support and give life to the community. If one faction of society is struggling to make humanitarian choices while another segment is inconsistently making choices - some beneficial and some harmful in nature - trust becomes a casualty of the struggle.

Swedish-born philosopher, Sissela Bok, in her 1978 book entitled *Lying: Moral Choice in Public and Private Life* wrote at length about the essentials of trust.

> "Trust is a social good to be protected as much as the air we breathe or the water we drink. When it is damaged, the community as a whole suffers; and when it is destroyed, societies falter and collapse… Trust and integrity are precious resources, easily squandered, hard to regain."

Understanding the value of trust, however, requires a complete look at the advantages and disadvantages of trust. Developmental psychologist Erik Erikson studied the stages of human development and identified trust vs. mistrust as the first stage of psychosocial development. Our first two years of life, according to Erikson, are developed through the satisfaction of our most basic human needs. We need nourishment as well as love and attention and how we learn trust is dependent upon how these needs are met. If we grow up to be trusting individuals with a realistic sense of caution, we find that we can strike a fair balance between trust and mistrust with regard to vulnerability and prudence.

We learn who we can trust and who we cannot trust by carefully observing their decisions and their ability to choose life. Associate Professor of Philosophy at the University of Western Ontario, Carolyn McLeod explains,

> "The social goods of trust are linked with the individual goods that concern moral maturity and cooperation. These social goods include the practice of morality, the very existence of society perhaps, as well as strong social networks. Morality itself is a cooperative activity, which can only get off the ground if people can trust one another to try, at least, to be moral. Yet to be able to make meaningful attempts in this regard, people have to be somewhat morally mature, which can only come from a moral education grounded in trust."

Being a trustworthy individual requires an effort to make consistent moral decisions that respect the value of life. If we found ourselves in a life-threatening situation, who would we want to make a decision for us, someone who makes life-affirming choices, or someone who does not?

Forgiveness – People make mistakes; it is part of our freedom of choice to make mistakes so that we may learn from them. Sometimes people make choices that are detrimental to their well-being or to the welfare of others. Some of these bad choices and mistakes are founded in the unfortunate circumstances of poor upbringing and dysfunctional families. People can make terrible choices for any number of reasons: desperation, fear, self-preservation, mental health issues, or what we find most difficult to understand – the harmful influences of society.

Why should we forgive people for their terrible choices? What life-benefit could there possibly be for absolving someone for the damage they have done to us or to society? The medical staff at the Mayo

Clinic in an article on Adult Health defines forgiveness from a health standpoint and offers a list of benefits of forgiving others:

> "Generally, forgiveness is a decision to let go of resentment and thoughts of revenge. The act that hurt or offended you might always remain a part of your life, but forgiveness can lessen its grip on you and help you focus on other, positive parts of your life. Forgiveness can lead to healthier relationships, greater spiritual and psychological well-being, less anxiety, stress and hostility, lower blood pressure, fewer symptoms of depression, and lower risk of alcohol and substance abuse" (mayoclinic.com/health/forgiveness).

A key to forgiveness is the ability to distinguish between *understanding* and *condoning*. These two words are not synonymous. By understanding that an abuser probably grew up in an abusive environment we can understand the behavior and forgive him/her, but we do not condone it. It is still important to hold someone accountable for their mistakes and to require that they take responsibility for their actions, but in order for us – individually and as a society – to grow and let go, and to forgive, we must be willing to relinquish bitterness, hatred, resentment or a need for vengeance. An individual and a society cannot heal while carrying the heavy load of indignation. Resentment and holding grudges are impediments to growth. Whether one has been injured by a person, a group, an institution, an ideology or a system, the act of forgiveness is the first step toward healing. In her book, *Left to Tell*, Rwandan-Genocide survivor Immaculee Ilibagiza writes,

> "I knew that my heart and mind would always be tempted to feel anger--to find blame and hate. But I resolved that when the negative feelings came upon me, I wouldn't wait for them to grow or fester. I would always turn immediately to the Source of all true power: I would turn to God and let His love and forgiveness protect and save me."

Understanding helps us to find common ground with one another so that we can work toward reconciling the areas that separate us. The life-choice is to forgive; it is a kindness, a gift of benevolence, so that we can move forward and enrich the world, rather than deplete it by holding on to barrier-behaviors of enmity and aggression. This need for understanding must be extended to ourselves; we must recognize our own mistakes and ask to be forgiven. Offering our forgiveness to others is as vital as asking for their forgiveness in return. Experiencing the gift of forgiveness – to be forgiven – is a healing salve for our well-being. When it comes to forgiving ourselves, it's important to remember that excusing our behaviors and mistakes is not the same thing as forgiving. Excusing requires nothing; there is no action involved, therefore, nothing changes and nothing grows. Forgiveness requires something; it requires an action from us. There is something we must do to amend the situation. Actions stemming from forgiveness foster growth and healing.

Regrets vs. remorse – While having no regrets in life is a good approach to living, *no regrets* should never be confused with *no remorse.* Everyone makes mistakes and poor choices. To state that one has no regrets means that at some point a lesson has been learned and remorse is a part of that lesson. To live one's life without regrets means to acknowledge a mistake or poor choice, to make amends where possible, and to revise the habits that lead to those same mistakes and choices. It is very important to be grateful for the opportunity to mend and heal the injuries that poor choices incur.

Mercy - People love the idea of mercy – it resonates with the concept of receiving another chance, a clean slate and the opportunity to start fresh. Who doesn't feel grateful when they receive mercy instead of punishment? If one is pulled over for speeding and the police officer administers a warning rather than a ticket, who doesn't breathe a sigh of relief? If a student experiences some type of family trauma and could not submit an assignment on time, is he not grateful for the teacher that extends the deadline? Judges, police officers, teachers, supervisors and parents are not the only ones who have the power to show mercy. We all have it within us to endow someone with the gift of kindness that can bring someone hope.

One of the most compelling scenes in literature that demonstrates the life-giving power of mercy is found in Victor Hugo's *Les Miserables* after Jean Valjean, the main character, is released from prison, has nowhere to live, nothing to eat and lands on the doorstep of a rectory inhabited by an old bishop and his housekeeper. Having to carry an ID card that identifies him as a convicted thief, Valjean has little hope of starting a new life, finding a job, and living a decent lifestyle. When the bishop invites Valjean into his home for a meal and to rest for the night, Valjean sees no other choice than to steal the silverware so that he might eat again tomorrow. When the bishop awakens and discovers Valjean in the midst of stealing the silver, Valjean responds from a primal survival instinct he'd nurtured in prison; he assaults the bishop and makes off with the silver, only to be apprehended by the gendarmes the next day and returned to the rectory. Valjean, having lied to the officers that the bishop had given him the silver, is now presented before the bishop to be formally accused. The bishop was well within his right to indict Valjean for theft and assault and send him back to prison, but he chose to show mercy. He confirms Valjean's story that he'd given him the silver, and gives him all he has so that he may start a new life, then speaks to the broken man in confidence:

> "Do not forget, ever, that you have promised me to use this silver to become an honest man.' Jean Valjean, who had no recollection of any such promise, stood dumbfounded. The bishop had stressed these words as he spoke them. He continued solemnly, 'Jean Valjean, my brother, you no longer belong to evil, but to good. It is your soul I am buying for you. I withdraw it from dark thoughts and from the spirit of perdition, and I give it to God!'"

As the story progresses, we find that Jean Valjean makes good on his "promise" and that the act of mercy endowed him with the ability to start a new life, worthy of the kindness he had been shown, and in turn, he shows mercy and kindness to others. Mercy, a life-giving force, has the power to facilitate charity. The choices emanating from mercy are twofold. One can offer mercy to another as a gift of charity, but the receiver has a choice as well – to accept the gift and make it worthwhile or to misuse the gift and devalue its potential. A driver who gets a warning can be more careful; a student can submit a higher quality assignment for having received more time; or they can both squander the gift and return to ineffective behaviors. Mercy brings together the qualities of forgiveness and trust. It has the power to create the ultimate win-win situation.

Compromise – Around 1259 BC Ramses the Great, Pharaoh of Egypt and King Hattusili of Syria, signed the very first written peace treaty in history, ending the strife between the two countries that had lasted for over one hundred years. In this ancient treaty, both sides conceded territorial demands and pledged themselves to peaceful relations. At the start of the truce, Ramses pronounced that "There is no reproach in reconciliation when you make it." Compromise is a life-giving force that stems from a willingness to work together rather than clinging to the destructive effects of discord. Bearing all of this in mind, it is critical to remember that while we seek to establish peace, the life-affirming foundations of morals, values and standing up for what is right and life-bearing should not be forfeited. Some things should never be compromised. Just like trust, it is important to discern a good compromise from a damaging one. When life is what is compromised, a darkness of civilization develops, where people are lost and scrambling to find their way back to life. We don't compromise another person's life to save our own skin. We look out for each other – genuinely. As in the old proverb, *we don't throw the baby out with the bath water.* Compromising, or throwing away what is good in life, to make peace with the destructive elements of society can lead to catastrophic results. We don't compromise with leaders of genocidal agendas. We don't compromise with tyrants and despot whose methods of governing eradicate human rights and freedoms. We learn to temper freedom and liberty – to find that delicate balance between making choices that serve the individual *and* humanity.

The human conscience is a fundamental component of compromise: *What are we willing to give up?* Morals, values, ethics are at the heart of a functional society, and the human conscience struggles to integrate these fundamental principles with respect to diversity of cultures and belief systems. The National Defense University addresses Strategic Leadership and Decision Making by emphasizing the importance of ethics with regard to compromise and social integration,

> "To behave ethically is to behave in a manner that is consistent with what is generally considered to be right or moral. Ethical behavior is the bedrock of mutual trust. A society with irreconcilable differences on fundamental issues will be torn apart. Hence, it becomes a moral obligation of public officials to engage in give and take, working toward compromise in the policies they develop" (http://www.au.af.mil).

A workable compromise preserves the integrity of morals, values and ethics. As individuals, when we deal with others in an agreeable way that preserves fundamental human rights, we develop a mutual harmony that allows for each person to retain life values according to the commonalities of beliefs, traditions and customs that support them. This type of compromise and social integration supports the value of life from a human rights perspective. Just like a family, a society needs to strive for functionality. No one wishes to live in a dysfunctional society that abuses, neglects, or destroys its members and their basic human rights.

Healing - Strive to be a healer. Everything, at one time or another, in our world needs healing. Our physical and psychological needs often require some care, nurturing, and healing. Relationships need healing; at present, the way society functions could use some healing practices, and our relationship with God, which may be suffering from a bit of indifference neglect could benefit from healing. Approach people, situations, places, nature, and the spirit with gentleness, compassion, and charity. Find a peaceful solution to situations, find ways to preserve someone's dignity. Refrain from the divide-and-conquer example we've observed from politicians. Inconsistencies, double-speak, and contradictions confuse the healing process. Show respect for everyone you meet because they are human. Work at understanding how others feel, or why a destructive situation has reached a certain point, and identify ways for healing. Allow people to heal in mind, body, and spirit by not damaging their self-esteem but by guiding them with gentleness and patience. Suggest kindly; nurture goodness, and always *defend life.* Remember that the value of the human potential is to reach the highest good through love. When struggling with difficult choices, use life as the measuring stick – how can I heal myself, how can I heal others, how can I heal this situation, how can I heal the progression of life, and not inhibit its growth?

With the inclination of modern medical science to treat many ailments with pharmaceutical drugs and invasive treatments, many people have turned to alternative, and more natural forms of healing. According to the American Holistic Medical Association,

> "Holistic medicine is the art and science of healing that addresses care of the whole person - body, mind, and spirit. The practice of holistic medicine integrates conventional and complementary therapies to promote optimal health, and prevent and treat disease by addressing contributing factors. Holistic healthcare practitioners strive to meet the patient with grace, kindness, acceptance, and spirit without condition, as love is life's most powerful healer" (holisticmedicine.org).

The human person has been endowed with an amazing power to heal from within. Treating the whole person so that the root of the illness, injury, or problem is addressed, and not just the symptoms, is a life-giving choice. Modern medicine can integrate these attributes of healing and not focus primarily on external, and possibly more dangerous, methods. Consolidate the wellspring of life-giving behaviors.

The Peacemaker – Human beings make choices, sometimes by using words and sometimes through actions, that offend, cause injury, destroy trust, end relationships, or take away a person's hope – these poor choices may be unintentional or purposeful. The peacemaker finds ways to initiate healing instead of perpetuating the conflict. In order for the life-giving process of healing to occur, the peacemaker understands the five steps needed to begin the restorative process:

- acknowledgement of the problem – understanding what hurts and *why*
- compassion – the ability to offer the loving way out
- reparation – what will it take to negotiate peace
- forgiveness – the ability to let go of the grievance
- change – a commitment to not repeating the action or making the same mistakes

One of the snares of being a peacemaker is the temptation to make excuses without intentionally meaning to do so. Excuses don't actually heal anything, they tend to have a bandage effect that brings about "peace for the moment," but soon the persistent problem surfaces once again. By making excuses and scapegoating, some peacemakers find that they are willing to do anything to achieve peace. But, true and long-lasting peace comes from acknowledging the truth and taking responsibility for it. Confronting the difficult truths and rectifying the core problem has a more permanent effect, and respects the integrity of the individual. Despite the criticisms lodged against theologian, philosopher and missionary doctor, Albert Schweitzer, his work as a peacemaker was based on love and the brotherhood of humanity, that we're all connected to, and responsible for one another. What connects us is *life*. In his 1923 Preface to *Civilization and Ethics*, Schweitzer wrote:

> "True philosophy must start from the most immediate and comprehensive fact of consciousness, and this may be formulated as follows: 'I am life which wills to live, and I exist in the midst of life which wills to live'... Mankind had to choose to create the moral structures

> of civilization: the world-view must derive from the life-view, not vice-versa. Respect for life, overcoming coarser impulses and hollow doctrines, leads the individual to live in the service of other people and of every living creature. In contemplation of the will-to-life, respect for the life of others becomes the highest principle and the defining purpose of humanity."

When we recall the lyrics of Jill Jackson and Sy Miller's song "Let Peace Begin With Me" we understand the fundamental principle that in order to be a true peacemaker, we must make peace within ourselves first and foremost. We should work to make peace with our past mistakes and the mistakes of others that hurt us. Being a peacemaker requires that we begin by healing the wounds within each of us. The world itself is showing visible signs of woundedness. The world needs *life* support. Working together *consistently* for peace is the kind of life support that can heal our world. We can make peace within ourselves by diminishing anger, hatred, jealousy and all the barrier-behaviors to peace. We can bury these impediments to wholesomeness once and for all. Living life as a true peacemaker means that you are at peace with yourself. Use the five pathways to peace: acknowledgement, compassion, reparation, forgiveness and change. Achieving this level of peace helps one to make life-choices and minimize destructive patterns of behavior. There is no peace to be found in self-destructive behavior, and once we acquire a level of inner peace, we can begin to find ways to bring peace to others and to the world around us.

Life thoughts

> *Let there be peace on earth,*
>
> *And let it begin with me.*
>
> *(Jill Jackson)*

Barrier Behaviors to Life-Choices

In 1516 St. Thomas More wrote: "You must not abandon the ship in a storm because you cannot control the winds... When you cannot turn to good, you must at least make as little bad as you can."

Non-Life-Giving Choices and Behaviors

Every behavior is a choice. We always have the choice to act in a way that is courteous, loving, kind, and life-giving, but there are many times when we feel we have reasons to act otherwise, and we may feel that these reasons are justified. When we have experienced a deep and abiding hurt, when we have been the victim of a crime or atrocity, or have been treated unfairly, our vision of goodness is bruised and may blind our decisions unless we find a way to forgive and to heal, and to move forward. Hurtful actions constitute a barrier to life-giving avenues. Harmful choices and actions stunt growth. These actions may damage situations or relationships, or even unravel something that is good. They are called *barrier behaviors.*

Indifference and Atrophy – The attitude that if a problem doesn't directly affect me I don't need to do anything about it does not promote a useful pattern that results in fruitfulness. If certain problems persist in our families, communities, or culture, the indifferent choice, while seemingly inactive, is persistently damaging to society and inhibiting the actions that may improve life. Indifference is a slow and painful death – of a relationship, of a community, and of a culture. The features of indifference which destroy relationships can be applied to the social strata as well.

Dr. John Grohol, Founder and Editor-in-Chief of *World of Psychology* explains, "When we've closed ourselves down in a relationship, we've shut off caring. We've shut off growth. We've shut off learning. And we've shut off life" (psychcentral.com). In order to revitalize the world around us we must open ourselves up to growth by working to be the change we wish to see in the world; we must learn how we can be a functioning member of society by actively getting involved – if each person in the world fed just one other person besides themselves (or their own families) the problem of hunger would be resolved; there are endless ways we can participate in *life* beyond living our own. We can take part in a universal cultivation of life.

Recognizing the problems that need to be addressed is a positive step in the right direction, but if our concern is limited to allowing others to tackle these problems our interest is auxiliary at best. *Someone needs to fix this problem* isn't an active strategy on our part. By asking ourselves *what life-giving decision I can make to fix this problem*, we participate in a more pro-active approach. If, upon rising, we ask ourselves *what life-choice can I make today?* we realistically sets the ball into motion. Apathy, laziness, or procrastination in our personal habits is not life-giving force. We may wrongfully think that we are taking care of ourselves by indulging in procrastination and by not employing self-discipline techniques, but the direct result of non-action is anxiety, frustration, or the worst possible form of destruction which is despair. Implementing the dynamics of fruitfulness has its roots in one of God's first instructions to the human race.

When God speaks in the first chapter of Genesis, shortly after creating man and woman, he gives them a definitive command: "God blessed them, saying to them, 'Be fruitful, multiply, fill the earth and subdue it. Be masters of the fish of the sea, the birds of heaven and all the living creatures that move on earth'" (Gn. 1:28).

When God saw all that he had made and declared it to be good, he put us in charge; his desire is for us is to multiply *all* that is good. Multiply life, increase the work that he began; it's not just about having children, though we have the capability and responsibility to share in procreation, he wants us to give life to everything we do on earth and to make it good. Breed good things by making more good things. Make life-giving choices and watch things grow. Multiply the good we see in the world. If we see something good, make it better. If we see something that has the potential to be good, feed it. Put an end to indifference – care enough to increase the good in the world – cultivate prosperous goodness. To do nothing is stagnation and eventually turns to decay. Atrophy is a sign that something good wasn't nurtured, cared for, or cultivated. All of us have been blessed with certain gifts or talents and we have an obligation to give life to them. These unused blessings may suffer, weakening the creative spirit within us. Each day we have a brand new chance to use our gifts and talents to make the world a better place. By applying our gifts *when* they are needed we promote growth in the world – it's not up to just some people, it's up to all people. By living up to our highest human potential, we can help others to live up to their highest potential as well, and, as a result, the world will benefit.

Hubris – Self-esteem is achieved through learning, growing, experiencing and loving. We achieve a level of self-esteem by overcoming obstacles, understanding our mistakes, correcting ourselves, and loving ourselves enough not to cause ourselves further harm. Self-esteem is healthy and life-giving. Hubris is not self-esteem. It's a deceptive shadow that obscures self-esteem and inhibits growth; it does not allow us to see our mistakes clearly, and it enables us to continue making the same errors again and again; it blocks our ability to understand others – why they might be damaged and how they can be helped. Hubris is an obstacle to sharing in someone's joy and often results in petty behaviors that damage relationships. As a barrier-behavior, hubris thwarts our ability to see the possibilities of improving ourselves. Whereas self-esteem recognizes areas where we may improve and helps us to envision growth possibilities, hubris accepts arrogance as an appropriate status-quo; it is a dangerous form of stagnation based on an illusory sense of well-being. Hubris can be identified when something good takes on the look of arrogance, self-righteousness, or when something wishing to be recognized as good takes on the veil of pride. Hubris allows us to confuse integrity with self-deceit. Integrity necessitates a humbleness of spirit so that we can work toward loving others beyond ourselves. Self-deceit soothes us into thinking that only individualism, and self-centered thinking and self-love are important. Integrity requires some degree of humility so that we can reach a higher level of humanness. Christian minister and author, Rick Warren once said, "Humility is not thinking less of yourself; it is thinking of yourself less." It's truly okay to observe areas within each of us that can use some help. Digging up and discarding the infertile soil of hubris and planting the gentle seeds of humility can yield an abundance of opportunities to care for the world around us. In order to love to a greater capacity, we must extend love beyond ourselves.

> "Oh, how the ego rebels against the thought of humility. 'If I'm humble, I'll be a nothing. I'll vanish! I must be distinguished, different, better than! Only by standing out will I have an identity,' it screams. We in recovery have felt the stinging reprisals from our fellows when we listened to our ego and let it have its way. Today, we have found a better way. Humility, like so many other concepts in recovery that at first seem like weaknesses, turns out to be one of our greatest strengths. By thinking about ourselves less, a truer identity emerges, a more peaceful and fulfilled sense of self that comes from being of service to and from connecting with others"(Michael Z, Empowerment Life Skills Coach and is a registered Marriage and Family Therapist Intern - selfgrowth.com).

Humility generates love, while hubris imposes limitations on its ability to thrive. For example, a relationship where one person cares more about himself than about the other person is a relationship that isn't going anywhere and will soon hit a wall. A life-giving relationship flourishes when the parties involved find ways to make love prosper by giving to the other person and reducing hubris.

Deception and Betrayal – part of the problem with deception is that we often fail to realize we're not fooling anyone but ourselves. We may believe that we are successfully deceiving others, but the only one deceived by that notion is the self. Lying to ourselves makes it so much more difficult over time to recognize any truth at all. Lying breaks down trust and weakens relationships and once trust is gone completely, there is no viable relationship. Deception is destructive – it kills any healthy association, whether in the workplace, in the family, in friendships, or in our world view. Perhaps we have become desensitized to the harmful effects of deception because of the media, politics and the entertainment industry. Deceptive tactics used to push through an agenda is not limited to one party or another, it has become commonplace. In our nation, trust is being devoured by the deceptive maneuvers of the government. We have become a culture that tolerates deception as long as it's employed for the "right" reasons. Many find it reasonable to overlook deceptive practices as long as the leadership in place advances the agenda that serves a popular schema. Refined rhetoric or sugarcoating objectives that destroy life-giving choices is not the equivalent of effectiveness.

Deception is promulgated and tolerated in many fields, such as medical and psychological research, environmental concerns, foreign policies, business and different forms of media. When one decides in business for example, that it's okay to say whatever is necessary to achieve a desired outcome, where does one draw the line? Is it okay to be deceptive in a small business but not a large corporation? Is it okay for protestors and activists to employ deception of their own because the end justifies the means? Is deception a reasonable tactic in the entertainment industry because the lines between truth and fiction are already faint? Deception is not limited to an outright lie, but is also perpetuated by partial truths. When the media draws public attention to only one side of a story by exposing only one angle, or by burying a story altogether in order to highlight another, this practice is just as deceptive as printing or broadcasting misinformation. Ethics need to be restored to the media. Just as pharmaceutical companies that promote a drug that has shown effective results in treating an illness must disclose the harmful side effects, so should the media be held accountable for information intentionally left out of a story. Modern media and politics would have us believe that some things are just more important than the truth. When is it tolerable for politicians to lie? What constitutes an acceptable lie? What is more important than the life-giving nature of truth? When we withhold the truth from anyone we perpetrate a crime against their basic human rights to make decisions based on facts, not what someone would have us believe. Deception is just another form of theft. In the Daily Halacha, Rabbi Eli J. Mansour writes,

> "The Tosefta in Masechet Bava Batra lists seven categories of theft, and mentions at the top of the list, as the most grievous form of thievery, the sin of "Geneivat Da'at," which literally means "theft of the mind," referring to deception. The Ritva (Rabbi Yom Tov Ashbili, Spain, 1250-1330), in his commentary to Masechet Chulin, writes that deceiving another person transgresses a Torah violation. According to the Ritva, the verse "Lo Tignovu" ("Do not steal" – Vayikra 19:11) refers specifically to this form of "theft," and thus a person who deceives another violates this Torah prohibition. This is also the position of the Yerei'im (by Rabbi Eliezer of Metz, France, 1115-1198), in Siman 124. Others, however, maintain that deception transgresses a Rabbinic edict, and not a Torah violation" (thedailyhalacha.com).

Most assuredly, when we deceive a family member, a friend, a co-worker or boss, a neighbor, or the general public, we have stolen from them *the truth*. Denial is a negative energy that draws the very life out of clarity and the ability to discern good choices based on the truth. The kinds of ambiguity that result from contradictions, rejecting honest attempts at good works, scrambling so many issues so as to camouflage an agenda or cause divisiveness are a threat to relationships and society. The life-choice to rectify these injustices requires that we make amends by coming clean, reveal the truth and apologize. Standing by your intentional deceptions is destructive, not only to your own life, but to countless people who may be affected by them. Credibility is rapidly becoming an endangered species. It's time to reevaluate our standards – if deception is unethical, it is *always* unethical.

Betrayal – when we betray someone's confidence or trust, we rob them of hope. This type of unfaithfulness in maintaining good relations has profound detrimental effects; its duplicity banks on the expectation of loyalty while it works in opposition to safeguard the relationship. Betrayal is an accelerated destroyer that works deeply at the core of our ability to trust. While most people have learned to tolerate a certain amount of deception, white lies, and fiction because they can identify some purpose behind it, betrayal has the power to terminate future opportunities by taking advantage of trust, or disregarding it altogether. Betrayal lodges itself more deeply in memory and has farther to go in the recovery of trust. The more intimate the relationship, the more betrayal has the capacity to kill something necessary for growth.

Insatiability - is a life-draining trait. Never having enough of anything isn't a life-giving force. Insatiability begins to consume what is good to the point of excess – until there is little or no good left to enjoy. Insatiability siphons the well of opportunities, depletes the spirit, and demoralizes the human person. By striving for excess, we become less human, and less life-giving. The force of insatiability extends to eating which causes obesity and a host of unhealthy conditions; it reaches into our relationships where life-giving intimacy can suddenly take a back seat to feelings of being used; it distorts our vision of needs vs. wants and gives way to extreme materialism; and it thrives on resentment which hinders us from ever feeling grateful.

Greed, in all forms, prevents us from growing as healthy, appreciative individuals. When pointing out that someone else is being greedy – be careful that this accusation doesn't stem from envy. Neither characteristics are life-affirming and both should be recognized as barrier-behaviors that inhibit healthy choices. Moderation allows us to have what we need and share with others. It augments goodness, and gives us the choice to appreciate our good fortune and support others that can benefit from it, too.

Role confusion – An extreme barrier to life-giving choices - I am vs. I have

This section, for a moment, may sound like an English lesson, but communication is dependent on language and so is understanding. Let us, for the sake of argument, take a look at two of the most common English verbs we unconsciously use to understand ourselves: *to have* and *to be*. In addition to helping other verbs, the verb "to have" is a verb that shows possession. It only shows action when it is used in conjunction with other verbs. The verb "to be", however, refers to a state of being. Because of our indiscriminate usage or understanding of these two verbs we may suffer from slight role confusion. Possession and being have distinctive qualities.

"I have parents", for example, may have nothing to do with an action on my part – it is the result of their actions. However when we shift the role identity to the state of being (to be) "I am a daughter" it now requires something of me. Being a daughter means more than being a female child to someone. In terms of defining the role of being a daughter, it requires some action on my part. What do I do that earns me the title? Depending, of course, on what I do and the degree to which I do it, we can begin to add adjectives. I am a good daughter because I take care of my parents. I am a daughter because I give something back to the people, or person, who raised me. I am a daughter because I show my mother or father that I love them. I'm not who I am because of what I have, I am truly who I am because of what *I do*.

An adjective is a word used to describe a noun – it is not the noun itself. A noun is a person, or a place, or a thing. How we define ourselves is completely different from how we describe ourselves. We are not adjectives – we are persons. Adjectives describe a changing sense of what we are at any given moment. The more permanent sense of identity lies in *who* we are not *how* we are. We have roles, not because of what we have, or how we feel, but because of what we do. How do we define ourselves as a person? I am – someone – because of what I do.

I am a mother – not because I have given birth to offspring, but because I do things that the role requires of me; I love my children, I take care of them, I work to provide them with a quality of life, I give to them and make sacrifices for them – all of these actions constitute the work it takes to maintain my role. When we begin to define who we are separate and apart from what we do, we may become confused, and a barrier of role confusion results. I am married has a greater meaning than *I have* a spouse. I am married means I work, together with my spouse, at marriage, a bond that requires many actions on a daily basis, the greatest of which is to love.

Verbs are the action words that give the noun some depth or meaning. By defining ourselves by what we have instead of what we do, it becomes more difficult to understand who we are. I may *have* a disorder, but that's not who I *am*. I may *have* a disability but I *am* greater than my disability because of what I can *do*! I may have tendencies that compromise my choices, but who I am is defined by my ability to overcome those tendencies, disorders and disabilities. I have the power to do great things despite any challenges because I am not a weakness; I am not malady; I am not a syndrome. I am a human being that may have struggles, but because I am human I have strength, and courage, and the ability to conquer the disadvantages that threaten to keep me from being the best person I can be. Because of my humanity, I can aspire to something greater than the "disability" or "disorder" or "tendency." Humans recognize this extraordinary potential and we tend to honor and respect the courageous examples set by people such as Nick Vujicic, (author of *Unstoppable*) a man born without limbs (see his website at http://www.lifewithoutlimbs.org/), Helen Keller, Michael, J. Fox, Stephen Hawking, and so many more. These incredible people have demonstrated that they are indeed greater than any setback, more impressive than any special physical or mental need, and more vigorous than any human weakness. We should always be careful how we define ourselves and make choices to support the best possible "me" that one can be. A human being is greater than a label because of human potential. When no one interferes with our potential, when we refuse to succumb to excuses and accept the challenge, there is nothing we can't do – we have the choice to be fully human!

When we begin to look more closely at who we are and how we define ourselves, which nouns we use to identify our roles, we must look even more closely at what we do to earn that title. How is my role defined by my actions? For example,

I am a Christian, Jew, or Muslim, because I do...
I am a teacher, a doctor, a firefighter, because I do...
I am a friend, because I do...

A role requires more than just one action. It necessitates a dedication to many actions. I am a teacher (not just because I *have* a teaching degree) but because I learn from information and experiences; I communicate this information in creative ways to my students, I guide them; I counsel them; I listen to them; I give them a forum where they can best learn and grow; I exchange information with them; I recognize I have as much to learn from them as they do from me; I give them the best of myself, and so on... Being a teacher is more than just giving homework. The more we do, the better we are, the more we work to reach our highest potential – the more room there is for growth and development.

First and foremost, we are human beings before we work at any chosen roles in life. What is it that makes us human? What do we *do*? We are capable of specific actions apart from nonhuman living creatures. The sheer number of differences between humans and other species can fill volumes, but for the purposes of this argument, we will focus on our ability, as humans, to love and to choose life. This constitutes a greater claim than the kind of "love" we receive from animals and their instinct for survival. This contention is dependent upon the discussion of the highest form of love as explained in an earlier chapter.

Love and life have far different meanings for humans than they do for animals. Though some would argue that their pets show more loyalty and affection than some human beings (and they're not wrong), pets have innate limitations as to how much love and affection they can choose to demonstrate. Human love has infinite potential. Life has unlimited possibilities. Animals possess the ability to show traits of love to their caregivers such as affection and loyalty - and these are *qualities* of love, but human love has the ability to grow beyond certain traits, with richer promise on a far greater scale. By our sheer human nature, we may choose to love to this greatest degree, whether or not we choose to do so is another matter. Love is more than a feeling, love is action. Yes, love is a verb, but it is one which covers many actions. To be fully human is to show complete affection and loyalty for our entire species, for every creature, for the earth, the universe, and for God. To place any restrictions on our ability to love is to limit our humanness. Our role as humans is to love and to make those choices that allow love to grow. When we experience role confusion and fall short of seeing how much more loving we can be, we accept our labels as a sufficient status, and the barrier behavior that affects every aspect of our lives inhibits our ability to be genuine, and to grow beyond its limitations. As humans, our role requires that we breathe life into the world, to enrich it with the best possible choices that benefit all of humanity and everything that has life and potential. Recall the Maslow hierarchy, the human is more than the basic, bottom-level needs. The complete human is self-actualized.

Rejecting values - When we become resolute in the kind of thinking that focuses strictly on the self we begin to view things like ethics, morals, and values as a threat to what we desire. Secular ethics, though they purport to be based on reason, logic, or "moral intuition" and separate from religious foundations, contain many of the same tenets of religious-based morality; they are simply reworded, and wording is subject to change. Secular ethics also find that they are confronted with opposition if a person is opposed to *any* type of proscribed regulations. In other words, secular ethics are no more effective in governing behavior than religious-based morality, and are no more immune to resistance.

The secular value system is based on the ideals of fairness, honesty, respect, courage, responsibility and caring, not unlike the life-giving behaviors previously mentioned in preceding chapters. Every system, secular or otherwise, encourages human behavior to be guided by the principles that benefit all people, not one person alone.

The Muslim faith asserts the following rules of justice in the Qur'an:

> "{5:8} O you who believe! Be upright for Allah, bearers of witness with justice, and let not hatred of a people incite you not to act equitably; act equitably, that is

nearer to piety, and be careful of (your duty to) Allah; surely Allah is Aware of what you do.

{49:9} And if two parties of the believers quarrel, make peace between them; but if one of them acts wrongfully towards the other, fight that which acts wrongfully until it returns to Allah's command; then if it returns, make peace between them with justice and act equitably; surely Allah loves those who act equitably" (http://www.introducingislam.org).

The Hindu faith affirms social justice in the following:

"Ethical actions calculated to promote social welfare is enjoined upon all who are identified with the world and conscious of their social responsibilities. Without ethical restraint there follows social chaos, which is detrimental to the development of spiritual virtues" (http://www.hinduism.co).

Among other social, moral and strictly Judaic laws, the Law of Moses encompasses the 10 Commandments in (Ex. 20 or Dt. 5):

"1. You must not have any other god but me. 2. You must not make for yourself an idol of any kind or an image of anything in the heavens or on the earth or in the sea. 3. You must not misuse the name of the Lord your God. 4. Remember to observe the Sabbath day by keeping it holy. 5. Honor your father and mother. 6. You must not murder. 7. You must not commit adultery. 8. You must not steal. 9. You must not testify falsely against your neighbor. 10. You must not covet your neighbor's house. You must not covet your neighbor's wife, male or female servant, ox or donkey, or anything else that belongs to your neighbor."

Christians inherited the Ten Commandments from their Jewish beginnings, but also uphold the commandment that Jesus Christ added when he said, "'Love the Lord your God with all your heart and with all your soul and with all your strength and with all your mind'; and, 'Love your neighbor as yourself'" (Matthew 22:39, Mark 12:30, Luke 10: 27, John 13:34).

Values and standards of living have come to us from many belief systems and they reinforce the idea that we are responsible for our conduct, not only out of self-preservation but for the sake of all. Upholding core values has a purpose that goes beyond maintaining social control or public order; it is a form of justice that depends on love and life whose ultimate goal is peace. There is very little peace to be found if everyone were to construct and live by their own set of values without regard for others.

Materialism – The problem with thinking of materialism as a condition that only applies to the wealthy is that this type of judgment limits us from recognizing it in ourselves. Doesn't everyone have the ability to be materialistic? The wealthy are not more materialistic than the average person, they simply have the means to exaggerate it. Materialism is a state of mind that, by definition, means to devote oneself to material possessions at the expense of spiritual or intellectual values. It is not confined to a particular social or economic class.

Materialism is not only about *having* material possessions; it is also about *wanting* material possessions. You don't have to be rich to *want*. If we remain focused on having life the way we want it, even if it means making other things less important, then we are forgetting to put others first before our own desires. We are physical beings that must, by nature, attain a homeostatic environment which meets the needs of life; we need to remain physically and emotionally healthy; we have the need for safety and security. Meeting our needs is not materialistic; focusing on our wants is a slippery slope into the mindset of materialism. We rationalize our materialistic mindset by focusing on those who have the means to take it to a higher level.

It's critical to remember that we are not only physical beings, we are also spiritual beings. If we were physical creatures alone, there would be no purpose for the upper levels of Maslow's hierarchy. If it were so, we could be perfectly happy with meeting all our needs at the very bottom levels, but we have a compelling need to reach greater heights than our physical natures demand. We have a burning desire to achieve so much more in life than finding something to eat each day. It is easy for us to confuse the spiritual and the physical desires. Having more of *something* should make us happy. For this reason, those who have reached the heights of material wealth show no evidence of having found supreme happiness, and those who have devoted their live to the well-being of the spirit through love and charity have found the depths of joy.

Confusion and inconsistencies can plague any facet of life. Multiplication of good does not equate with materialism. Giving life to our ability to help others does not mean we are focused on hoarding for our own benefit. We need to increase goodness, talents, gifts, and blessings in order to share them. True materialism cares nothing for others and stands in direct opposition to spiritualism. We have a spirit within us that wishes to thrive. Our spiritual needs – love, belonging and esteem - work toward self-actualization. The more time we spend on wanting things, the more we are pulled away from wanting God, or a higher meaning of life. Materialism is a choice. It is very difficult to work to satisfy both materialism and spiritualism to their greatest potential since they exist at opposite ends of the spectrum. What lies in the middle is the ability to increase the good to use it for improving the world. Materialism is a barrier to reaching a better self when it is focused on the self alone. Multiplication of goods is a benefit to the world and should not be confused with greed.

Accelerated destroyers

Excuses and blame – these behaviors inhibit growth by shifting responsibility. A person who makes excuses or blames one's parents, bosses, bad luck, continually remains stagnant and never moves forward. Choosing life means to relegate these rationales to the waste bin – they are non-productive.

Dr. Timothy A. Pychyl, Associate Professor of Psychology at Carleton University, Ottawa, explains that when "Our values and beliefs don't align with our action… rather than using this tension to signal the need for change, we take the path of least resistance and excuse ourselves." Dr. Pychyl attributes this trend to a "pathetic path of least resistance."

> "… because we don't want to face who we really are with these choices. We'd prefer to believe something very positive about ourselves (a pro-environmental attitude for example), so when we act opposite to it (failing to make a pro-environmental behavioral choice), we don't want to face that this choice now defines us. Instead, we strategically reduce the dissonance by lying to ourselves. This is living in bad faith. Living a lie" (psychologytoday.com).

Making choices that promote harmony between our beliefs and our actions is a tremendous challenge. Making excuses is a barrier-behavior to living a harmonious life. The twin sister of excuse is blame. Blaming others, rather than taking responsibility for our own actions is also known as scapegoating. The Scapegoat Society, founded in the UK to address the effects of scapegoating defines it as

> "… a hostile social-psychological discrediting routine by which people move blame and responsibility away from themselves and towards a target person or group. It is also a practice by which angry feelings and feelings of hostility may be projected, via inappropriate accusation, towards others. The target feels wrongly persecuted and receives misplaced vilification, blame and criticism; he is likely to suffer rejection from those who the perpetrator seeks to influence. Scapegoating has a wide range of focus: from "approved" enemies of very large groups of people down to the scapegoating of individuals by other individuals. Distortion is always a feature" (scapegoat.demon.co.uk).

When we work to make better choices, it is a conscious decision to recognize the obstacles we place in front of ourselves that keep us from reaching our full potential, whether those obstacles involve making excuses or placing blame. When one begins a sentence with "I can't because…" one is not exploring all the other choices that may be available. In doing so, we have essentially limited our choices because the excuse or the blame can offer a path of least resistance. Once a habit is formed that allows us to make excuses for ourselves, for someone else, or with regard to a problem, we find that we can repeatedly make the same excuses again and again and nothing ever changes, nothing heals, grows, or blossoms. Excuses and blame constitute an end unto themselves.

Anger, Hatred, and Revenge

Anger is a valid, natural response to a personal, emotional injury, but it's not meant to be stockpiled. Holding on to anger severely limits choices and possibilities When we cling to grievances, even if we have good reason to be angry, we find that we begin to say *I'm not going to do this because… I'm not going to speak with… I'm not going to have anything to do with…* "I'm not" becomes a barrier-behavior with an endless litany of restrictions, often resulting in choices that impede the potential for healing and life-opportunities. If lodged deeply within us, it begins to control us and evolves into hatred which often turns into a burning desire to inflict harm on the offender. Before anger reaches the point of hatred, resentment, bitterness, and retaliation, one has the choice to express anger in a healthy and positive way. By using appropriate patterns and language to vent anger, a solution to the problem may become possible and life-affirming alternatives may open up new and unexpected avenues for growth. Sustained anger can dismantle good relationships, good prospects, and good efforts. When anger and hatred lead to revenge the possibilities for destruction are frightening as vengeful patterns can escalate and lose control.

Aggression has a way of inhibiting progress. Whether one employs passive aggressive behavior or active aggression the result is generally to forestall movement in a positive direction. For example, an apology that is met with contempt halts any further advancement toward reconciliation; a lack of response to a goodwill gesture discourages future expressions. There are very few true pacifists in the world, but for those who don't fall neatly into a category of passive or active aggressors, it is evident that the neglect of making a life-giving choice can be just as damaging as making a choice without regard for possible outcomes. When one exercises their right to make an individual choice that compromises the well-being of society, it is essentially a challenge to the progress of goodness, and it is a form of aggression that quietly undermines the human race in its ability to reach its full potential. When one persists in self-directed decision-making that opposes a higher standard, it is a quiet act of aggression that forces the hand of a moral society. In such cases, the perpetrator is either ignorant of his actions or so thoroughly ingrained in self-directed thinking that when encountering redirection, it is seen as a threat to their livelihood and subsequently accuses others of aggression without recognizing their part in facilitating it.

When these aggressive behaviors are allowed to continue they ultimately lead to a tit-for-tat pattern that has no peaceful solution. Peace has never been achieved by allowing for unlimited individual choices. It's an age-old desire to do whatever we wish without incurring consequences; and that's just not how it works. Many people wish to pursue life on their own terms without respect for life itself, and they do so aggressively in one form or another - any hindrance requires retribution. We mustn't even the score by adding insult to injury; we can only discover peace by lessening the emphasis on the self. Vengefulness and aggression have no place in peaceful coexistence.

The New Testament gives us a classic outline for the life-giving choices in the fifth chapter of Matthew when Jesus instructs us:

> "You have heard how it was said: Eye for eye and tooth for tooth. But I say this to you: offer no resistance to the wicked. On the contrary, if anyone hits you on the right cheek, offer him the other as well; if someone wishes to go to law with you to get your tunic, let him have your

> cloak as well. And if anyone requires you to go one mile, go two miles with him. Give to anyone who asks you, and if anyone wants to borrow, do not turn away. You have heard how it was said, You will love your neighbor and hate your enemy. But I say this to you, love your enemies and pray for those who persecute you; so that you may be children of your Father in heaven, for he causes his sun to rise on the bad as well as the good, and sends down rain to fall on the upright and the wicked alike. For if you love those who love you, what reward will you get? Do not even the tax collectors do as much? And if you save your greetings for your brothers, are you doing anything exceptional? Do not even the gentiles do as much? You must therefore be perfect, just as your heavenly Father is perfect" (Mt. 5:38-48).

Jesus Christ is plainly promoting more life-giving options. An eye for an eye puts an end to future life-giving choices by recognizing that vengefulness escalates, nothing is resolved until someone puts a stop to retaliation. Peaceful options encourage healing; it is the option in which no further harm is done. Love does not settle scores. It leaves options open. On the contrary, hatred seeks to punish with cruelty. Hatred is a choice; it comes from within and acts like a cancerous growth that leads to the death of love within us. Hating what is wrong with the world doesn't make it go away – hate *feeds* what is wrong with the world. By loving our enemies and working to heal the wounds that separate us from one another we forge a new path toward healing. Love is a healing force because it seeks to forgive injuries through understanding. Buddha reiterated this idea of letting go when he stated that "To understand everything is to forgive everything."

Revenge seeks only to payback an injury – it cares nothing for understanding, and can often render a situation irreparable. It is complicated by, not one, but two bad choices. Revenge can bring an end to any relationship. While on the surface vindication may appear to make us even, we come to dwell in the sphere of pain where the opportunity for growth is extinguished, rather than opting for the healing solution of forgiveness. Forgiveness is the act of pruning away the hurts in life while offering us the chance to grow and blossom without the burden of retaining the injuries we have suffered.

John Michael Talbot explains,

> "... forgiveness does not condone unrighteous behavior, but it does forgive it, and empower others to overcome it. Nor does it mean in enabling negative behavior. But it does constantly call everyone back to the positive wonders of God."

Returning good for evil is the best course of action against injury; and offers the life-giving response when true justice is the desire to make things right again. Adding injury upon injury kills the spirit, the person, or the hope for peace.

Enabling – is an accelerated destroyer because of its power to widen the path of least resistance. The pattern of enabling may unconsciously include the habit of making excuses or scapegoating. When one begins a sentence with, "I'm not making excuses, but..." and then proceeds to do so, one is in effect renouncing a healing path. By making excuses for ourselves or someone else who is behaving poorly, we counteract the healing options that lead to atonement. When dealing with people who have alcohol or addiction problems, the worst possible approach is to enable them – to accept their excuses, to look the other way or to blame someone or something for the problem. Enabling an addict gives life to the addiction and ends the life of the addict. Conversely, to support an addict means to end the life of the addiction and give new life to the addict. Supporting someone means helping them to face the truth and to make better life-choices. To enable someone means to help them deny the truth and make death-choices. Enabling removes a person's right to take responsibility and choose life.

Violence and Assaults – Violence destroys more lives than any other single force on earth. When violence is perpetrated against the self or others it constitutes a destruction of human dignity and life. Assaulting someone's good name is a violence. Assaulting one's way of life, religious beliefs, character, innocence, livelihood, well-being, freedom, opportunities, and dignity is a violence to basic human rights. Violence is not limited to physical assault from one person or one group of people to another. Violence can be the act of objectifying the human person, demeaning a person's life to a "lower function" rather than a higher potential. When one defines another's purpose by objectifying them, it is a barrier to that person's ability to discover their own purpose. When anyone or anything threatens a person's home, commits unlawful imprisonment, enslaves another human being for labor, sex or other crimes, subjects them to inhumane conditions, it is a violence that destroys the very fabric of society. Whenever the value of a human life is downgraded to its convenience to another, all human life is imperiled. The barrier-behaviors that rouse violence and assault on human dignity include hopelessness, intolerance, anger and fear, frustration, failure, disappointment, and limited thinking; that life-options are not an option.

Violence is a choice that takes on a destructive life of its own; it descends into a downward spiral that ultimately culminates in the death of something or someone. Child abuse, domestic violence, violent crimes such as rape, pedophilia, school shootings or other shooting rampages in public areas, all have their common roots in a choice to perpetrate an act of cruelty upon others because at some point the perpetrator was a victim to some type of violence as well and the necessary healing never occurred. Violence can also be the unfortunate result of mixed messages where an act of aggression is tolerated in one area and penalized in another. If humanity concurs that violence is wrong, then it is *always* wrong.

Selfishness – A group of women, sitting in a café, began lamenting about their husbands' shortcomings – the topics ranged from general complaints of poor listening skills, to watching too many sports but finally the women agreed that their husbands shared a core trait in common – narcissism. One of the women spearheaded the definitive problem by saying that "Everything is always about him, his ideas, his needs, his day at work, his goals, his everything. It's never about me."

Another woman asked, "Would you be happy if everything was about you?" Married people find out very quickly, that in order for a marriage to work, it has to focus on *us as a couple*. The "me vs. you approach" is the beginning of the end.

At the extreme, narcissistic behavior is a dyed-in-wool inability to see anything from a perspective outside of one's own. A true narcissist simply has no ability to empathize, to listen, to understand, or to appreciate boundaries. But most people are not narcissists. What many people find difficult, however, is to see the fine line between taking care of oneself and being selfish. To be truly life-giving we must love ourselves, but love others more; we must take care of ourselves while thinking of the needs of others; we must make decisions that make life better for everyone including ourselves.

Selfishness is a barrier-behavior that stands in the way of life-affirming decisions because kindness and charity are halted on our own doorstep. A person with selfish habits is self-focused and self-motivated with most decisions aimed at satisfying a bottom-level need. Selfish behavior can cloud a person's ability to see when they've made a mistake that has injured another and consequently find it very difficult to make amends. One of the most damaging aspects of selfish behavior is that gratitude becomes a casualty of their attitude. When selfish behavior takes over a person's mind-set, there is a sense of entitlement that disables their ability to feel grateful for what they have. If I only take care of my own needs and my own self, I don't need to be grateful to anyone else. Selfishness feeds on indulgent habits that evolve into insatiability. How can I be grateful for what I have if I don't have enough yet? Envy seeps into the mix while looking at the world through a selfish lens; we always look at someone who has more and we feel entitled somehow to exceed beyond another's good fortune.

When one settles into a selfish mode of thought there is the sense that no one can ever do enough for *me*. It's quite the opposite of *I would like to find ways to do more for others*. These thought patterns are not life-giving but destructive, because suddenly one finds that relationships begin to suffer, work performance is sacrificed, and dissatisfaction becomes a deeply rooted outlook. A person whose thoughts and behaviors are self-directed finds it difficult, if not impossible, to be a well-spring for the living, rather they become a bottomless pit of need, and what they need soon clashes with the needs of others. If everyone behaved selfishly, and no one thought of others first before themselves, the world would be a place of true torment. In order to promote a sense of worth rather than a selfish attitude, one must look outside of oneself.

When the barrier behaviors turn into habits that we tolerate in our lives, we begin to lose self-respect and forfeit our dignity. It becomes easy to use people, to hurt them, and even to damage our own lives. The very best way to combat the destructive effects of barrier-behaviors is to get into the habit of choosing life over choosing destruction. Find the life-choice in every option. It may feel good to make an excuse for the moment, to blame someone, to seek revenge or to follow a seemingly easier path, but that good feeling evaporates as soon as the excuse is no longer accepted, there is no one left to blame, the vengeful act has disastrous consequences or the easy path becomes a slippery slope to death. Avoid the barrier-behaviors to life-giving choices by looking at the bigger picture by seeing life-options and *choosing life.*

St. Francis of Assisi, a man gifted with the vision and understanding of the choose life paradigm, lived in the late 12th and early 13th century, a precarious time when many life-threatening forces such as war, poverty, disease and corruption were rampant. The prayer attributed to him most beautifully underscores the effects of life-giving behaviors over those that deplete the human spirit. It is a cherished testament to the life-giving principles because in each phrase of the prayer, the appeal is for the help needed to make the life-giving choice over the destructive choice:

> *Lord, Make me an instrument of your peace. Where there is hatred, let me sow love. Where there is injury, pardon. Where there is doubt, faith. Where there is despair, hope. Where there is darkness, light. Where there is sadness, joy. Oh Divine Master, grant that I may not so much seek to be consoled as to console, to be understood as to understand, to be loved as to love. For it is in*

giving that we receive; it is in pardoning that we are pardoned, and it is in dying that we are born to eternal life.

Life thoughts

In St. Francis of Assisi's prayer there are choices throughout the verses where he is asking for the help and the grace to make the right choices, the choices that give life and not death. There are times when we most definitely benefit from making the choice to die to our old habits so that we may live in the love and spirit that nourishes and gives life. Avoiding confusion and inconsistencies is a must to choosing life.

It's Not Easy Being Green

"A man's character always takes its hue, more or less, from the form and color of things about him" (Frederick Douglass).

One morning, a teacher decided to take her second grade class outside to combine reading time with snacks, rather than keeping the children inside on a lovely day. The children were eager to enjoy the fresh air and sunshine and in order not to lose this rare privilege they promised to attend to the lesson while enjoying some juice and a batch of homemade cookies prepared by their teacher. Once the lesson was completed and snacks were eaten, it was time to clean up and return to the classroom. Since preschool, the children had been ingrained with the rules of throwing their trash away, and then lining up at the door. By second grade, it's a habit. On this particular morning, one child, distracted by a chipmunk scampering toward the bushes, forgot to throw his juice box away and started for the door. Within moments, another child keenly pointed out the forgotten juice box, but before the child could reach for it, the wind had carried it away. Instantly, two dozen children fled in the direction of the airborne juice box in an effort to retrieve it. The group effort was a success.

The point is, if we conscientiously form habits that love, nurture, and care for the earth, we become more instinctively proactive in making environmentally healthy choices, and more acutely aware when others do not, either because they are distracted by other issues, or because they've forsaken the habit since the second grade. Re-ingraining the habits that safeguard our individual choices and recognizing the impact they have on the world around us on a regular basis makes us more attentive to areas that need the most help. However, for it to work, it must be a group effort.

To our current knowledge there is no other planet in our solar system that supports life as we know it. The planet Earth is unique in its beauty and sustains each and every living thing that inhabits it unconditionally. It is abundant with life of various species, forms, shapes, colors and genetic makeup. As humans, we have been given dominion over this gift from God, the Creator of all life. Dominion means we have authority over this planet – a very serious responsibility to nurture it with loving care. The bottom line is that we have an individual as well as a collective responsibility to maintain the life of this planet by caring for it like a conscientious guardian, father, mother, or friend by making decisions that choose life for the well-being of everything that exists on the planet. Each time we make a choice that endangers the well-being of our planet, or fail to care for its inhabitants, including ourselves and the plants and animals with which we share it, we place all life in peril. Abusing precious resources, by using more than we need (remember there is a difference between needs and wants), we demonstrate a propensity for making destructive choices.

John McConnell, the founder of International Earth Day, in his "77 Theses on the Care of the Earth" urges us to

> "recognize that there is in the human spirit a desire for meaning in life, and to recognize that the present crisis of our planet. The greatest virtue or moral imperative is the care rejuvenation of the Earth and securing the right of all people to its natural bounty."

Each choice we make affects the life, security, and welfare of the Earth's inhabitants, both now and in the future. This endeavor is not the responsibility of government agencies alone; caring for the Earth is an individual responsibility as well. With the abundance of environmental agencies in place, we have somehow relinquished our personal duty to care for water, plants, animals, the air we breathe, nature in general – and each other. For example, if we feel we have done our part by electing politicians that care about the environment, then our work is done. The reality is that as we walk away from the voting booth we are faced with unlimited opportunities to make life-affirming choices for our planet.

In *Ethics: Opposing Viewpoints*, author Laurie DeMauro quotes John McConnell,

> "People should behave ethically to preserve the environment. Neglecting and abusing the resources of the planet has endangered all life on Earth. Mutual trust benefits the common good. Strive for peace and care of the Earth. Reclaim the Earth to free its people from fear of war and want. Peaceful care of the planet requires the dedication of all humanity. The time has come for all of humanity to take charge and take care of the planet… this requires ideas and attitudes geared to this purpose."

It is critical to recognize that each choice we make has an impact on the world in which we live. Conserving, recycling, reusing, preserving what we have around us ensures that we may have it longer for ourselves, our children, and their children. Do we fix things or throw them away – not only with regard to material things, but with relationships, jobs and communities? There are many actions – *life-giving actions* – that we can utilize to improve the world around us. The principles that we apply to environmental responsibility can also be applied to dealing with others and with ourselves. Making concerted efforts in our consumer habits from the vehicles we buy, to the temperature at which we set our thermostats, as well as re-evaluating our needs vs. our wants to benefit others, can not only extend the life of this planet's resources but also help us to coexist more amicably. Becoming environmentally conscious and well-informed consumers, neighbors, friends, family members, co-workers and citizens requires that we take our stewardship of *all* life more seriously.

Working to be *green* forces us to take a look at all our choices – energy choices, transportation choices, food choices, gadgets, clothing, the chemicals we use, and all the things we utilize in daily life, as well as what to do with things once we're finished using them. We must become more knowledgeable by having a realistic understanding of the goods and services we use, what we waste, and the actions we take to rejuvenate the Earth. The simplest way to make life-choices sometimes boils down to making the choice that which will cause the least amount of harm.

Being *green* goes back to the idea of respect. A healthy respect for natural law is as important as a well-grounded respect for civil law. When we violate a natural law there are consequences just as surely as disobeying a civil law. Being green means we understand the consequences of our behaviors and we freely choose to respect the laws of nature and morality. Having respect for nature and the environment by safeguarding natural resources and humanity is a vital step to take to heal the world in which we live. Consider the idea that being truly green involves having a universal respect for nature as well as natural law, bearing in mind that we should respect the human race as a part of nature in keeping with the natural laws that govern life. Being a *green person* means having the self-respect needed to promote a natural lifestyle that reduces the amount of harm that we inflict on ourselves. Being a *green person* means we consistently choose life as a way to live. We refrain from any harmful habits that could potentially harm our existence. Being a *green person* means we shake hands and make peace with natural laws. A *green person* understands the benefits of being fully human which includes making life-giving choices, eradicating the routine habits that keep us from being the best *green person* we can be. This concept requires that we apply the same principles to ourselves as we do to the planet. By living to a higher standard, we can achieve a better self, and a better world.

The reciprocal relationship requires that we recognize that the environment supports all life on the planet therefore people have a responsibility to preserve *life.* If we want to preserve the environment, we must begin by preserving *the human.* We have the power to make environmentally human choices that support life by applying the same eco-friendly principles to our own lives. The human environment respects the total human.

Choose not to pollute the air in the environment - Just as pumping harmful pollutants into the air reduces the quality of the air we breathe, so does filling our thinking and our actions with negativity hinder our ability to make positive, healthy choices. Once we begin to tolerate a pollutant as "normal" we begin to make polluted choices. At the same time that our lungs, filled with chemicals or nicotine, fumes, and exhaust emissions are subject to airway constrictions and lung damage, filling our lives with violent images, pornography, aggression, materialism, and egocentrism can diminish our positive decision-making abilities.

If we wish to breathe cleaner air, we must implement stricter measures to purify the air. Likewise, if we wish to lead happier, healthier lives we must make conscious, more self-disciplined personal choices not to pollute our bodies and minds with anything that makes us less than fully human. We must refrain from all pollutants that affect us morally, ethically, spiritually, socially, and emotionally. Physical pollutants that limit, change, or destroy our body's natural processes, and alter our natural body rhythms, have serious toxic effects just as psychological and emotional pollutants can have the same noxious effects. Learning to tolerate harmful emotional pollutants such as individualism and dissension, or worse, redefining them as harmless does not change the impact they have on our well-being. We have witnessed the effects of pollutants in water and air, radiation, and toxins on the physical health of our population and there has been extensive research to illustrate the devastating effects of these pollutants on our offspring as well. The same holds true for negligent, dangerous, or immoral behaviors - our children have been placed in harm's way by our tolerance for harmful media, films, games, and social interactions with an increase in frequency and variety of juvenile crimes, bullying and school shootings.. The time has come to give more thought to choices that pollute the environment of our lives and the lives of our children.

Choose not to use harmful chemicals, pesticides, hazardous wastes that harm our resources - As previously discussed, many of the harmful choices we make can have a devastating effect on our ability to lead healthy lives. We must avoid harmful chemicals that damage, not only the environment, but our health. We need to abolish the use of narcotics and find ways to limit the use of pharmaceutical drugs that diminish our capacity to be fully functioning individuals or which cause mind-altering damage that affect our decisions. Choose the options that promote life, not inhibit it. An unhealthy dependency on chemicals can ultimately damage our quality of life. Giving in to ads about the benefits of non-organic substances and by redefining them as helpful, we relinquish control over our decisions to use any number of substances. Whenever your body is telling you that you need more of a particular substance, you are no longer in complete control of you decisions.

Choose renewable energy for humanity – Acknowledging that the source of life is a loving Creator, not merely a random occurrence of energy helps us to understand that love exists for a reason. Love supports life. Life, in turn, supports love. When we make personal choices that align our wishes with living love, there is no limit to the loving possibilities. This type of renewable energy is rooted in a Divine love that extends infinitely in all directions. We know when we are acting in harmony with the will of the Divine because love is the governing behavior, and life happens. When all of our decisions are guided by love, and in a life-giving direction, we find that we don't deplete our lives of healthiness; we increase it. However, each time we make a choice that rejects an opportunity to love, to choose life and core values, we feel it – it hurts. Feelings of sadness, anger, jealousy, pettiness, lethargy… are not renewable energy. When such feelings arise, replace them with the renewable energy feelings of charity, joy, serenity, loving kindness, generosity, compassion, understanding, and so on… These feelings renew or rejuvenate us. Be a *green person* by healing your relationship with God, by redirecting your hearts to love as He loves us, and to re-energize your life by uniting it with His will for love and for life.

Choose to be Eco-Friendly by nourishing an environment that doesn't harm life - Making personal choices more carefully means that we don't place ourselves in harmful situations, like remaining in relationships, careers, or living conditions that don't contribute to healthier living. Making the green choices to begin with means that we ask ourselves - is this marital, business or social relationship *green*? Can we make a green life together, one that promotes life-giving routines? Is this a green career; is my labor life-giving; am I at the mercy of non-life-giving policies? Are my living conditions green? Is there trust in my life? Am I free to make life-giving choices? Does faith play a role in helping me to make better choices?

What is needed to nourish life is an understanding of the ecology of human nature. Building on the concept of human ecology – a sociological way of looking at how human beings interact with their environment – we foster an understanding of our humanness, and how we can reach a higher standard in our relationships at all levels. To be human is to understand that we have many relationships that require our best choices. A conscious awareness of our ability to make choices out of love and to avoid choices that place limitations on love is at the apex of our human ecology. With every choice we make we can choose to love and thereby give life, or we can choose to restrict love and diminish life. As a human being I can do things out of love that other species cannot – I can create and I can sacrifice; I can give and teach others to be charitable; I can rise above the person I was yesterday rather than making excuses; I can understand, respect, and observe the laws of nature and moral laws; I can continue to aspire to something greater despite any obstacles in my way; I can recognize my dignity as a human being and cherish this dignity in others; I can, by virtue of reason, select choices that benefit all of life; and I can identify with and acknowledge God that has given me all of these abilities and to use them wisely.

Choose sustainable living by reducing waste, respecting the natural balance of our resources and natural cycles - In our choices it is critical that we not overlook what is truly special about life, that we maintain a healthy balance without excessive behavior, and that we respect each stage of the life cycle by living up to the opportunities each one presents. Sustainable living means that each developmental phase of life is recognized for its potential, its uniqueness, and its worth. Each special time period in life should be given the respect it is due by cherishing its distinctive qualities, and by respecting the balance that is unique to each stage.

Childhood is the only time in life when innocence is possible. We should respect children by allowing them to sustain their innocence. They deserve to be protected from the responsibility that comes with understanding adult matters. Allow children to have the dignity of being a child by promoting the integrity of childhood. It is a special time in life because wonderment and anticipation are the gifts that precede the weight of understanding. The time arrives soon enough when difficult choices are encumbered by mature issues. We can ensure that children maintain a balance between growing up naturally and accelerated development by ensuring that mature themes are prevented from invading their lives – in educational curriculums, in the home, in entertainment, and in all forms of media.

The Tween Generation – Kay S. Hymowitz, educator and author of *Ready or Not: Why Treating Our Children as Small Adults Endangers Their Future and Ours* has this to say about the tween generation – that period of life between childhood and puberty (between eight and twelve):

> "... this group is leaning more and more toward teen styles, teen attitudes, and, sadly, teen behavior at its most troubling." From the way they look to the way they behave, "the tween phenomenon grows out of a complicated mixture of biology, demography, and the predictable assortment of Bad Ideas... they rely more heavily on others to tell them how to understand the world and how to place themselves in it... they are being increasingly 'empowered' to do this on their own, which leaves them highly vulnerable to both a vulgar and sensation-driven marketplace and to the crass authority

> of their immature peers. In tweens, we can see the future of our society taking shape, and it's not at all clear how it's going to work" ("Tweens: Ten Going on Sixteen," *City Journal*, Autumn, 1998).

Exposing children at a younger age to more violence in games and more sex in education has not reduced the tendency of children to engage in these behaviors at an earlier age. As a society, we have failed to respect the dignity of childhood. We can redirect this trend by choosing life for our children by allowing them to live the life of a child before they must, by nature, live the life of an adult.

Adolescence – The precarious time between childhood and adulthood is characterized by rapid growth, being inundated with life's lessons, and having to discern for oneself what is right, what is wrong, what to believe, and what to achieve. It's no wonder that teenagers are in a constant state of flux. Simply proclaiming to them that they are alright, despite the fact that they can now see for themselves that everything is not alright causes tremendous confusion. The adolescent population has always been better able to identify mixed signals more clearly than any other group. They hear one thing, and see another. They are taught to adhere to a set of principles but see that their role models choose otherwise. They have grown up with video games that tell them that it's okay to pretend to kill, but it's not okay to do it for real. The images in the games seem real enough. They've been taught that in some instances it's acceptable to kill an innocent person, but in other cases it is not. How can they distinguish between right and wrong when the rules are individualized? They have come to learn that if it feels right for you, then it's right – until suddenly, society tells them they have now done something wrong. There is great uncertainty and misunderstanding among adolescents for a reason – some of those reasons are perfectly natural and others have been created by a confused society.

As a society we can encourage healthy choices in our teenagers by teaching them to make life-affirming choices *consistently*. Teach them to scrutinize contradictory messages and follow the path that promotes life-giving options. Adolescents can benefit from the model that encourages a consistent chain of positive human development. If we wish for our adolescent children to bear the fruit of goodness, kindness, respect, honesty, etc… we must provide them with unwavering examples. There will always be difficulties, predicaments, tough choices, and frustrations in life, but helping our youth to recognize opportunities for growth in adversity is a sound, life-affirming principle that helps them to direct their energy away from destructive solutions.

Adulthood – That integral time period between the age when we are considered to be legal adults and the time when we can no longer care for ourselves presents us with the greatest opportunities for freedom of decision-making than at any other time in life. Adulthood is truly the most important time in our lives when making an inestimable number of choices is the fruit of our very existence. We should respect this particular time period in life by making the best choices that sustain life, our security, our ability to grow and make more choices and take special care with those choices that affect others who may depend on us.

This stage of life provides us with the greatest opportunity to achieve a healthy balance in living through the choices we make. Our adult decisions affect our choice of careers, family living, parenting, friendships, community living, general health, lawful citizenship, and spiritual growth. At no other time in life can we enjoy the amount of freedom we have to make our own choices, and it's vital to remember what Eleanor Roosevelt advised: "Freedom makes a huge requirement of every human being. With freedom comes responsibility." The more freedom we have, the greater the responsibility. As adults, we make choices every day that affect not only our own lives, but that of every living thing on this planet. It is a tremendous responsibility that should never be taken lightly. The ability to reach a general consensus among adults to foster choices that promote life will help to develop a social ecology that benefits everyone.

Seniors - The crescendo stage of life is distinctive for its wealth of experience, and its unmatchable ability to entrust the next generation with an archetype of living life to the fullest. The senior stage of living is remarkable for its ability to appreciate the features of all previous stages, and with this appreciation the ability to embrace the pinnacle of life with wisdom and dignity. Are there special challenges in this phase of life? Of course, but these "abilities" far outweigh any "disabilities" that come along. As with any stage, the senior phase has plenty of challenges and opportunities to demonstrate a life-giving design by upholding the best of what makes us fully human – to live to our potential each day, and to gracefully accept the changes that arise from one day to the next. Aging with dignity means that all the life-affirming values are upheld until our lives speak for themselves, and self-respect is sustained in every choice we make. Joe Brennan's site, AgingPositively.com offers this advice:

> "Self respect, self esteem and morale are some of the most important ingredients involved in dignity. There is no age limit at either end of the spectrum where these qualities are not needed. Because of the way society views the process of aging, we cannot expect to be treated as we would like to be. That does not mean that we are forgotten, or that we are seen as lesser citizen. I think that we have to change the way we see ourselves and the way we want to be seen as a very important part of society with something really worthwhile to offer."

Many senior living communities have adopted a lifestyle philosophy that focuses, not only on physical care, but on the *whole human being.* In this senior living framework, communities such as Erickson Living focus on a mission: "to change the way Americans view aging by consistently offering services and resources that make growing older something to look forward to." The wholeness of being human is as critical at this stage as it is at any other and can be addressed by quality health care for physical and psychological needs, by continuing an esteem-building approach to life by encouraging seniors to contribute to and build their own communities, and by fostering a strong sense of spiritual wellness. The totality of humanness does not diminish at the crescendo of life, it reaches its peak. Choosing life means we can help the aging to be fully human to the extent of their own personal abilities each and every precious day.

Conservation - Choose to recycle and reuse our resources – Using creativity to our benefit! If an area of our life isn't working out the way we'd like, rather than destroying it, how can we apply creative measures to keep what is good in our life but make it more workable? Recycle an area of your life that needs to be energized. Rather than ignoring a character flaw or remaining in denial about a problematic issue – confront it, take what is good and make it better, pruning away only that which is harmful. Healing is a conservation measure that we should utilize by making repairs to our brokenness. At times, we may find that we need help to restore our well-being. Could we benefit from counseling to help us discover creative options rather than destructive alternatives?

We can work to find ways to conserve relationships. If we feel that someone we know is losing their ability to remain positive, they seem to be collapsing or alienating people around them, we can look for ways to conserve the relationship rather than discarding it by helping them to seek the help they need. This might pertain to a loved one, a friend, an employee, or a neighbor. If we retreat from the person who needs help, they may feel isolated and begin to despair. Help them to see how they can recycle and renew their lives! Conservation is an effort that works against declination. There are people or situations that can bring us down and make us feel like we are sinking. To conserve our well-being, we must choose life by rising above these difficulties, by reaching for healthy living and not succumbing to the negative influences.

What our garbage says about us – Organizing Associates, Inc., a national consulting firm that helps businesses and clients to organize and de-clutter their personal space, works with clientele to analyze what should be kept and what should be discarded. They have found that people generally keep things that "they might need it someday… or still [has] use, or if it's something that makes them happy, or could bring joy to others in their family." But analyzing what people throw away is just as interesting. Are we throwing away things that might still have some use? Do all things become useless simply because we've had them for a while? What about *ourselves* do we throw away? Should we throw away values that simply don't fit into a modern world? Should we discard positive qualities of our character because we haven't been appreciated? Should belief systems that have true value be abandoned because they're "old-fashioned?" It's time to analyze what we are throwing away as individuals, and as a culture, that may still have worth, may still make someone happy, or that may be needed in the future? Productive change doesn't throw away the good along with the bad. It would be worth the time and effort to take a peek in our cultural trash bin and see if there is something in there that shouldn't be. If our culture is producing an extensive amount of media/entertainment/social waste, we should reexamine our reasons to create these harmful influences and discard those things instead.

Grow organic children – As a culture, we'd like to think that what we do to our own bodies hurts no one else; that taking care of ourselves has only a personal benefit. The truth is, what we do to our own bodies – smoking, drugs, alcohol, poor nutrition - affects our children. Human DNA is a composite of our ancestors' choices. At present, what we do to benefit our bodies, to keep ourselves healthy by eating nutritious foods and avoiding harmful substances, has an impact on our offspring and descendants. The National Institute on Drug Abuse reports that "various drugs of abuse may result in premature birth, miscarriage, low birth weight, and a variety of behavioral and cognitive problems" (drugabuse.gov). Further, the U.S. Department of Health and Human Services reports that

> "Children who experience either prenatal or postnatal drug exposure are at risk for a range of emotional, academic, and developmental problems. For example, they are more likely to: experience symptoms of depression and anxiety, suffer from psychiatric disorders, exhibit behavior problems, score lower on school achievement tests, demonstrate other difficulties in school" (childwelfare.gov).

What effect has the accepted practice of recreational drug use had on our children? We must consider the health of our children even before we begin to reproduce. A stronger commitment to healthy habits must begin during our growing years, and continue during adolescence and young adulthood. Poor nutrition, substance abuse, and lack of exercise are habit-forming behaviors and have long-range effects on the human race in general.

Organic children grow into organic adults. Growing organic children, however, goes beyond physical concerns alone; there are many emotional, social, psychological, and spiritual factors that contribute to the growth, well-being, and development of "organic children." Children are products, not only of heredity, but environment as well. How well our children develop psychologically, emotionally, socially and spiritually depends greatly on how-well equipped we are as parents to work through and confront the tough issues. Parents play a critical role in helping their children to grow up with openness to spirituality and a relationship with God. Tolerance of many religions does not mean we eliminate speaking about God; it means we help children to understand the diversity of faith, and the many ways people choose to worship him. Rabbi Sandy Eisenberg Sasso, author of several children's books on fostering spirituality in children recommends that parents,

> "Encourage the religious imagination in children... [by] reading and learning about your religious tradition, about faith. Live your faith. Talk about God... and let children join you in expressions of care, gratitude, and hospitality... by not being afraid of the conversation [about God], creating an everyday spiritual world — where symbols, rituals, objects are as familiar as Happy Meals and teddy bears, and where religious personalities and biblical characters are as commonplace as Mickey Mouse and Donald Duck, by telling stories and creating an environment where children get to tell their stories, by belonging to a community where people live the stories of faith. Children need coaches not just for

> soccer; they need spiritual mentors for life.... Making time for prayer, for silence...At quiet times, children give us a glimpse of something precious, eternal: their souls. They need intentional quiet to remain in touch with their spirit" (spiritualityandpractice.com).

Nurturing our children with a firm foundation in faith is step one in the ultimate challenge – to protect them from harmful influences. Spiritual foundations provide our children with the necessary defenses against the non-organic hazards to their mental health and well-being. There are many environmental dangers to physical health because of chemicals, but exposure to the harmful effects of mixed-messages, criticism, bullying, violence, discrimination, abuse, vulgar language, pornography, and the damaging effects of the media, entertainment industry, and many video games can also prevent our children from enjoying complete, healthy growth and development. Organic children have a stronger fighting chance to defend themselves against these perils by learning values firmly rooted in the life-affirming teachings found in the tenets of faith. Eliminating God from organic upbringing is like expecting plants to grow without sunlight.

Organic children learn to value life – they appreciate seeds that grow into plants, that living things need clean air, water, food, and respect for their habitat in order to grow. Organic children learn to value all aspects of human life – they learn to respect the seeds of human life from conception, that all people, regardless of age, sex, disabilities, religions and race are entitled to the protection of human dignity. We must teach children to love all human beings (even if we don't like what they do) and to be peacemakers by finding opportunities to heal each other. The most profound way we can teach our children about being fully human is to venture beyond education that only concentrates on the *physical* human. Being human is about more than how the body works; the names of the parts, and what each part is used for. It would be like teaching children the parts of a tree and how it grows without teaching them why trees are important. Organic children have a broader understanding of what it means to be a human being with all the potential for love and living life to the fullest by understanding why we need to choose to love and to choose life.

Anyone who has raised children or even worked with children understands that consistency is a necessary factor in teaching children right from wrong. If there are too many discrepancies in the information children receive they can become confused and have difficulty learning the message. Teaching children to make life-affirming decisions must be a harmonized endeavor. Our actions must be consistent with our words. We set examples by showing self-restraint when options do not promote life. In guiding them to make choices that support life, that encourage unity, promote peace, inspire growth, and fuel opportunities, we can help children to see the world through a more homogeneous lens. We cannot expect children to grow into individuals who work for peace if we teach them that some life has no value, that some people don't deserve chances, that making individual destructive choices doesn't harm life on this earth. Inconsistent messages undermine all the current value-based education programs and the evidence is in the violence we are witnessing in schools.

The National Association of Students Against Violence Everywhere is a group "devoted to community and school violence prevention programs including conflict management, crime prevention, service projects, more." This group, formed by students for the benefit of students, is committed to the idea of peace.

> "On a Friday night in 1989, a young man named Alex Orange lost his life while trying to break up a fight at a party. Alex could have been just another statistic of another young life lost to violence. But the following Monday, his grieving classmates gathered in West Charlotte Senior High School's cafeteria and vowed to organize against violence in Alex's memory. The group formed Students Against Violence Everywhere (SAVE), with the vision that all students will be able to attend a school that is safe, secure, free of fear, and conducive to learning… In just 22 years, SAVE has expanded from

> that first chapter in Charlotte, North Carolina, to over 200,000 members in over 2,000 SAVE chapters across the U.S. Today, SAVE serves youth in elementary schools, middle schools, high schools, colleges, and community youth-serving organizations in 48 states and several foreign countries" (nationalsave.org).

Teaching children to live their lives in an organic way requires a higher standard. Taking care of our bodies and our spiritual life is just as important as not littering or pumping harmful pollutants into the atmosphere. We must teach them to have an organic vision for the world that is free from violence – to be *green* in all areas of life, not just some of them. By guiding children to look out for each other, to share the same peaceful goals, and protect one another from harm, and by instilling the life-affirming values on a consistent basis is as fundamental as using sustainable energy sources. We teach them to recycle bottles and cans because they still have use, but allowing a grandparent to be tucked away without recognizing usefulness (even if that usefulness is to teach *us* to love unconditionally) contradicts the meaning of being wholly green. Children can be taught to see the bigger picture and value the ultimate goal for humanity – to choose life. We have an obligation to help our children see the world as an environmentally friendly place for all life and to make the life choices to accomplish it. Nature shows us how – Clean Air Gardening experts remind us that

> "Trees are like the lungs of the planet. They breathe in carbon dioxide and breathe out oxygen. CO2 is one of the major contributing elements to the greenhouse effect. Trees trap CO2 from the atmosphere and make carbohydrates that are used for plant growth. They give us oxygen in return. Trees also help to reduce ozone levels in urban areas" (cleanairgardening.com).

Humans are every bit as capable of turning something bad into something good. Return good for evil is an old proverb that has served humanity well for many ages. John Walsh, recipient of the Operation

Kids Lifetime Achievement Award, became a highly recognized crusader in helping law enforcement apprehend offenders who commit crimes against children after the 1981 abduction and murder of his son, Adam Walsh.

> "Viktor Frankl, a survivor of a Nazi concentration camp noticed people who survived were usually the ones who had good attitudes, despite their circumstances."Everything can be taken from a man but ...the last of the human freedoms - to choose one's attitude in any given set of circumstances, to choose one's own way" (Jean Hamblen, *Turning Tragedy into Triumph*).

Because there are times when people make destructive choices, there are opportunities to turn something tragic into something triumphant. A positive transformation is a life choice. We can take our example from plant life; just as trees are capable of taking harmful pollutants out of the air and releasing fresh oxygen, so too can humans take what is hurtful in the world and transform it into something good and life-giving. Our highest potential as human beings is to love; it is therefore through love that we can renew and refresh life around us. We can learn to breathe life into the world through loving choices.

Life thoughts

Harmony, balance, supporting the viability of our choices and making lifestyle choices sustain natural living. Why bother being green with the planet Earth if we fall short of becoming green humans that have a healthy respect for all life?

The Joy-Filled Life

"The true value of a human being can be found in the degree to which he has attained liberation from the self." (Albert Einstein)

If the greatest gift of human existence is the ability to make life choices through acts of love, then it stands to reason that when our actions work contrary to this purpose, we develop an uneasiness and anxiety that often lead to greater issues and possibly poorer decision-making.

Cognitive dissonance is a term introduced by Leon Festinger in his book *When Prophecy Fails*, which went on to throw the doors wide open for a new facet of social psychology. Cognitive dissonance causes one to feel distressed when their perceptions are in direct conflict with each other. For example, when our value system is in direct conflict with our actions, we feel a restlessness that nags at our conscience. People are generally motivated to reconcile this cognitive discord either by changing their values, or changing behaviors. An example of this would be when a person rationalizes a bad habit such as smoking, overeating, or compulsive shopping. The person has an integral knowledge that what they're doing is wrong, but may try to excuse or justify the behavior so that he doesn't have to feel bad about it. One way to accomplish this is through denial of the consequences.

Phil Barker, writing for *Beyond Intractability* (Univ. of Colorado, Sept. 2003) states that there are other ways in which people deal with eliminating cognitive dissonance or the discomfort associated with opposing or contradictory perceptions:

> "There are several key ways in which people attempt to overcome, or do away with, cognitive dissonance. One is by ignoring or eliminating the dissonant cognitions... adding or creating new cognitions...or by prevent[ing] it in the first place." (Phil Barker)

A society that values human life, but tolerates legislation, actions, and behaviors that damage, destroy, or devalues human life may find that it experiences cognitive dissonance on a massive scale and on an expansive cultural level, and for this reason the controversies over *right to life* cannot be resolved in the foreseeable future. In such a case, we find that we rationalize through media, entertainment, laws, educational curriculum and general propaganda. We want peace; we want social justice; we want economic egalitarianism; we want to put an end to oppression, poverty, and tyrannical violation of human rights because we view these as "goods" – but we continue to make certain individual choices that contravene social justice initiatives. The result can be a dissatisfaction felt at each level of our daily lives.

President Dwight D. Eisenhower, once said that "A country that values its privileges above its principles soon loses both." Our privileges are vitally important and only when they are in sync with our principles will there be harmony and peace. We make decisions with a goal in mind that to do whatever we want will make us happier; then, at some point, we look around us and try to understand why things are the way they are, why they aren't better? If this is the case, then it's quite possible that a disconnect occurs between our understanding of our decisions and how it affects our lives the world around us. For each individual a personal decision is a fraction of the whole, one small facet of all human decisions.

As humans, we are often strongly motivated by a desire to be happy. Even if we are not consciously aware of cognitive dissonance, we are in the habit of trying to reduce it through the rationales that, themselves, become a habit. When there is a clash between our decisions (which should make us happy) and the consequences (that caused some sort of problem), we resort to blame, denial, and excuses to assuage the conscience. Sidney Callahan in *Lured by the Spirit to an Ethical Life* (natcath.org) writes,

> "The innate capacity for the operation of conscience comes from the ability to freely choose between behaviors and the possession of enough intelligence to adopt standards of worth that transcend the self. We possess selfish drives of survival – competitiveness and desires for dominance. Built-in behaviors vs. thinking through choices can present us with inner conflict."

There is no doubt that, at times, the motivations that lie behind our decisions contradict our beliefs, attitudes and values, and in order to pacify the discomfort caused by these inconsistencies it is easier to change our beliefs, attitudes and values than to try to make life-affirming choices. When we allow barrier-behaviors to guide our decisions and to cloud our capacity for making loving choices, we are not living a life in harmony with the goal of peaceful coexistence. We can always find a rationale, a justification, an excuse, a reason, a plausible defense, or a logical pretext for non-life-affirming decisions, but they will eventually collide with another person's reasons, defenses, rationales, etc... It is only through consistent individual choices and a widespread effort among communities to make unified life-choices that we can begin to see a true and lasting change toward peace.

A joy-filled life is wrapped in love; the greater the level of love to which we aspire, the greater the joy. When our efforts to make choices are exercised at the highest level of love and choosing life, there is an innate joy that accompanies the realization of being fully and wonderfully human. Through practicing humor and unselfing, improving our communication and relationships, and making peace with God, we can achieve a joy-filled life that benefits us and the world.

Humor–This Emotional Life at pbs.org lists the positive and rewarding benefits of humor:

Physical benefits of mirth and laughter:

Increased endorphins and dopamine
Increased relaxation response
Reduced pain
Reduced stress

Cognitive benefits of humor and mirth:

Increased creativity
Improved problem-solving ability
Enhanced memory (for humorous material)
Increased ability to cope with stress, by providing an alternative, less serious perspective on one's problems

Emotional benefits of humor and mirth:

Elevated mood and feelings of well-being
Reduced depression, anxiety, and tension
Increased self-esteem and resilience
Increased hope, optimism, energy, and vigor

Social benefits of humor and mirth:

Bonding with friends and family
Reinforcement of group identity and cohesiveness
Increased friendliness and altruism
Increased attractiveness to others
Happier marriages and close relationships

A simple glance at this list of the benefits of humor reveals that this fundamental aspect of joy is a truly enjoyable way to choose life. Where one can identify the increases, improvements, enhancements and reinforcements toward happiness – there is a life-affirming directive.

Pain, stress, depression, anxiety, and tension – those feelings that deplete life – are reduced! Humor, according to researchers, elevate us in an "'upward spiral' to greater happiness" (pbs.org). Humor is a choice, a way to identify the beauty and joy in life-giving situations. It can soften the blow of devastation so that we aren't destroyed. Humor helps us to communicate a message that might be difficult, or helps us to improve morale in a challenging environment. Humor is an elixir for life.

Unselfing

"A man wrapped up in himself makes a very small bundle." --Benjamin Franklin

The ultimate paradox in life is that in order to be more fully human we must think of ourselves less and think of others more. A joy-filled life can be achieved by diminishing our attention to our own needs exclusively, and widening our consideration of others. We can discover joy when we look outwards by seeing that what we are able to do can make the world a little bit better. It would be delightful to see the newspapers filled with stories of good works rather than crimes, to view positive advances between political parties because they've both decided to initiate life-affirming legislation, to observe countries working together for peace, to find true hope that our children will have a better future because we are not usurping their inheritance for ourselves. But this cannot be accomplished as long as we remain focused on a philosophy of *doing what's best for me* on a personal level or shifting blame when there are inconsistencies between benevolent policies and destructive legislation on a societal level.

Unselfing means we work to curtail our barrier-behaviors; we think of ourselves just a little bit less so we can think of others more. If we are focused only on taking what we want for ourselves we are not adding anything to the world around us. This trend is non-life-giving because if our existence is predominantly focused on the self, growth of humanity is severely limited. When growth is focused on the betterment of all humanity, the possibilities are endless. Unselfing means we expand our lives – we make them bigger for a bigger and better world.

Unselfing also works to bring about healing – this is a powerful method to repair the wounds of being human. When a person encounters a sorrow, a tragedy, or a devastating loss, turning inward might seem like the right thing to do and for a while some privacy might help one to regain some perspective. In the long run, however, alienating others and isolating ourselves from the love of others prevents us from healing. We can build walls that separate us from further hurt, but these same walls can also separate us from feeling restorative love. Some find that determination helps them to cope with hurt or loss. They become entirely focused on taking care of themselves alone, but determination does not have the same healing properties as love. When we cut ourselves off from extending our love beyond our own needs, we stop growing. In a sense we are submerged in our feelings of sadness, grief, or despair. We may not even be conscious of these plunging behaviors because we are determined to handle everything on our own, but as time goes on we find that we can no longer see the brightness of anything good in the world and everything has a negative overtone. When we can no longer see the good in the world, we are no longer living life, we're merely getting through it. With every choice that adds to life, we diminish negativity, we strive for the positive.

The gift of choice has simultaneously been the joy and bane of our existence. We are able to freely choose between one option and another, but the right choice is often difficult to make, while the wrong choice, which is sometimes easier in the short term, can result in new difficulties down the road. Science and technology have improved many aspects of life and helped us to understand the physical world around us, but it was never meant to replace the spiritual aspect of life that helps us to understand our choices. Secular ideas and language have evolved in order to facilitate a more homogenous understanding of physical life, but they have a tendency to eliminate God from our understanding. Any time we eliminate something, we aren't seeing the whole picture. In order to be fully human we can expand our vision rather than limit it, we can look beyond our "selves" and our momentary needs, we can choose life and we can love, and we can teach others to do the same. We can guide our children to be fully human by creating and supporting life-affirming choices where they may find true joy, and not just recreation. We can help them to understand that life choices promote the kind of growth and change that benefit humanity, and that destructive choices encourage changes that benefit no one in the long run. There is greater joy to be found in unselfing and expanding our ability to love rather than focusing on short-term solutions that limit our power to do so. In the words of Supreme Court Justice, Clarence Thomas: "Today, now, it is time to move forward, a time to look for what is good in others, what is good in our country. It is time to see what we have in common, what we have to share as human beings and citizens."

Communication

An old saying reminds us that "we have two ears and one mouth and so we should do twice as much listening as talking." Reflective listening is a tool that fosters better communication skills by disabling some of the barriers that occur in the exchange of ideas. We feel a deep sense of joy when our ideas, thoughts and feelings are understood and validated. Reflective listening involves a simple two-step process: the speaker states his message, and the listener must repeat the message back to the speaker. Instead of thinking of how to reply, the listener must attend closely so that he can recap what was said. The speaker then knows whether or not his message was understood. This type of communication reduces the occurrence of misunderstandings, conflicts, and strife. By reducing the opportunities for frustration and discord, there is greater joy in communication. Reflective listening is often used in counseling because it allows the patient to have a voice, to have a forum where they are free to speak and be understood, and where they may encounter empathy – a life-giving form of compassion. Joy is anchored in being treated lovingly, so that one may treat others in a loving manner as well. Effective communication inspires joy. When our voices feel muted or isolated, we suffer from the hurt caused by indifference, disinterest, or rejection. Human communication is exceptional and unique in its ability to instruct and assist others, convey emotions, generate friendships, interact, and connect with one another.

Human communication can be a life-affirming choice that improves the world around us and cultivates a deeper sense of joy.

Choosing God

"I believe in the sun even when it is not shining, I believe in love even when I feel it not, and I believe in God even when He is silent." (An Irish Saying)

On April 8, 1966, the cover story for Time Magazine asked the question, "Is God Dead?" Eighty-four years after German philosopher, Friedrich Nietzsche's conjecture about the absence of a living God spawned various trends toward the "isms" that diminished the human need for his presence in our individual and collective thinking, the concept that "God is Dead" caught on as a popular, new idea. Does humanity need God now that we have advanced medicine that heals illnesses, discovered technology that defends and sustains our livelihood, and devised ways to control nature? Some would say we do not, while others would suggest that we need him more than ever because the complexities of our choices have clouded our judgment and we need some clarity and a renewed understanding of love. The simplicity lies in our ability to choose God. He is not dead simply because we have fostered the barrier-behaviors that obscure him. He has not ceased to exist as a result of our unwillingness to accept and acknowledge him. God has not been diminished as a result of our inflated selfness. God is not the one who turns away from us. From the beginning, he has chosen us, chosen life, and chosen to love us. We can choose him, we can choose life, and we can choose to love him – it has always been our choice. When we choose God, our creator, we can choose to create and not destroy. When we choose God who is love, we can better make the decisions that require more from us. When we choose God, we promote life.

Without a sincere love for God, have we placed limitations on our choice to love since we can choose to love only that which makes sense? The more reasons we offer for excluding God the more it seems we reduce the number of ways in which we can choose to expand love: I don't have to love something I cannot see; I don't have to love someone that has wronged me; I don't have to love someone that causes me an inconvenience; I don't have to love someone that has less than I have; I don't have to love someone that seems to love better than me; and I don't have to love someone that isn't just like me.

In *The Philosophy of Life* by Rosario Thomas, et. al., the idea of *living* relationships has a definitive quality, not only in our human relationships, but our relationship with God. "From a living relationship with God grows an awareness of the uniqueness and value of one's life and personal dignity."

Who can attribute the value of one human life better than God? Our fellow humans? Wouldn't that depend on their agendas, moods, disorders, opinions or unfortunate circumstances? Is there one who would wish that the value of one's life should be determined by flawed or troubled human beings?

William Hazlitt once said, "Love and joy are twins, or born of each other." Love is the reason for life and life is a good reason to show love. Every one of our choices matter. From the very beginning our choices have been life and death choices. It has been a central component of our humanity. If we align our choices with the choices that God makes, we sustain life, we advance it, we are able to *enjoy* it. If we choose to believe that there is no God, that he is not a loving God, that we are not created out of love, can we reach our maximum capacity for joy? Have we discovered our greatest potential to love? Humans, at their highest, are in awe of God, not obliterating him. Getting rid of God has not made the world better, and it hasn't made our choices easier. In turning away from "institutionalized religions" many people feel that they can still maintain a spiritual affectation toward God. However, it is quite possible that the connecting theme throughout institutionalized religions bears re-examination, because in turning away from religion, or God, we may be forgetting something very important – a *deeper* sense of love. The Golden Rule has found its way into many religious and cultural tenets:

- Judaism: What is hateful to you, do not do to your neighbor; that is the entire Torah; the rest is commentary.

- Hinduism: Do not to others what ye do not wish done to yourself. This is the whole Dharma; heed it well.
- Zoroastrianism: Human nature is good only when it does not do unto another whatever is not good for its own.
- Buddhism: Hurt not others in ways that you yourself would find hurtful.
- Udanavarga: In happiness and suffering, in joy and grief, regard all creatures as you would regard your own self.
- Confucianism: Do not do to others what you do not want done to yourself.
- Christianity: Do unto others as you would have them do unto you.
- Islam: No one of you is a believer until you desire for another that which you desire for yourself.
- Sikhism: Be not estranged from another for, in every heart, pervades the Lord.
- Baha'i: Ascribe not to any soul that which thou wouldst not have ascribed to thee, and say not that which thou doest not.

Having an all-inclusive respect for other religions and the way people worship God doesn't mean we become God*less*, it means we become God*full*. In one way or another, the divinely inspired message is clear – to love each other as you wish to be loved. It is from this epic truth that humanity can coexist peacefully and with joy, but it is a choice. We have the ability to choose joy in all our choices by making the positive decisions that increase opportunities for love. We can choose God because sometimes the ability to make choices that bring joy and goodness and life can be very difficult. Though it is more than evident that one of the most important gifts God has given us is free will, the ability to choose this gift would be meaningless without the gift of life. In the Lord's Prayer given by Jesus Christ, the phrase "thy kingdom come, thy will be done, on earth as it is in heaven" is a transcendent and powerful clue about making the decision to choose life. We associate the precept of God's kingdom of heaven as being a place that is filled with joy – it is about *life*. If God's will in heaven is about life-as-it-should-be, then "on earth as it is in heaven" is about making those choices that sustain a joy-filled life on earth. It's about choosing to love as we have been loved by God. In the words of self-improvement specialist, Dr. Wayne Dyer, "Heaven on earth is a choice we must make, not a place we must find."

Life thoughts

A joy-filled life strives for what is beautiful; it strives for what is organic to our nature – to promote life. We desire to live longer, healthier, more beautifully and more joyfully, and we desire to have love in our lives. Our desires are best realized when our choices are aligned with a universal spirit of life. Whenever we make a life-choice we can find delight in the knowledge that we have given life to the goodness of the world and that something wonderful can come out of our choices, that good can triumph over evil, that pain and suffering is not an end in itself, and that we took part in making something good even better. Someone once said, "It will be alright in the end, and if it's not alright, it is not yet the end." Choosing life ensures that things will continue until everything is alright.

Extraordinary Choices

"I find it as difficult to understand a scientist who does not acknowledge the presence of a superior rationality behind the existence of the universe as it is to comprehend a theologian who would deny the advances of science" (Werner Von Braun, Engineer, Rocket Scientist).

Science has helped to explain many things we once accepted on faith alone; it has broadened our understanding of nature and our humanity. The world view that nature, humanity, and creation are good gives science a firm basis and validation for its own existence. Scientists study the natural, physical world; they study behaviors and life; they study the intellect and knowledge itself; they study just about everything. Some aspects of science have taken bold leaps into the unknown so that we can better understand many things about ourselves and our relationship to the world with the hope of making better choices than we have in the past. With an increased understanding of DNA, organisms that cause diseases, medicines, bio-fuels, plastics, bio-control, and forensics, we have opened the floodgates to a world of new choices. However, with the burgeoning of scientific advances, many choices have become more complicated, rather than simplified. With all the scientific and technological advances that we've made, have we eradicated destructiveness, or have innovations offered us new ways to be destructive?

Georgia Governor, Nathan Deal, expressed the view that "Scientific advancement should aim to affirm and to improve human life." Protecting human life from such things as discrimination, selectiveness, and ethnic cleansing has given value to scientific advancements, but those facets of science that continue to promote inequity have caused unspeakable damage to scientific integrity. The value of human life is life itself. Dictating that certain conditions need to be met in order for life to have value reduces it to a subjective privilege and not a tremendous gift. If life were meant only for those whose existence were guaranteed optimal results - free from tragedy, illness, pain, suffering, hardships, and trauma, where would any of us be? It is as a result of this gift of life that, despite the human condition and all its problems, we have a greater privilege to become a vital force and give life to the world by the choices we make. As long as we have life, we have the choice to carry on its mission to generate and continue life.

French Renaissance writer and doctor, François Rabelais wrote that "Science without conscience is but ruination of the soul." It would be feasible to add that science that does not put life first is the ruination of humanity. When we are presented with the most difficult choices, those that leave us feeling that we have very limited options, where right and wrong are indiscernible, or our intellect and emotions are in direct conflict, it is precisely at those times that we need to employ the life-giving dynamic. The life-choice may not guarantee ease in the course of action; it may not be devoid of pain-staking results; it may require even more stressful decisions, or it may present as the more complicated choice, but it is the *only choice* that is rooted in love – the highest form of love that considers its impact on others and on the world. Love unlocks the doors to life-giving choices. Love of self is integral but should not be exclusive. *I love myself enough to make a life-giving choice but I also love myself not to be the one who is responsible for hurting another person.* It's not about living up to lofty ideals, or lowering our standards to make things easier; it's about living up to LIFE, and all of its challenges. It is the responsibility of the living to choose and to continue life.

Reverend Martin Luther King, Jr. once said that "Our lives begin to end the day we become silent about the things that matter." It is not only important for each person to make life choices but it's also critical for us to find a way to help others make them too. It's not a question of meddling; it's a responsibility to support others when they feel their choices are limited, to help them see all possibilities, including those choices that are life-affirming. Gerald Vann, in *Moral Dilemmas* reminded us that "Doing what everyone else is doing is not a good test for whether something is ethically right or wrong." According to this important principle, helping others to do what everyone else is doing, even if it is a destructive choice, is not ethically right either. When *we become silent about the things that matter* as a way to support someone and not guiding them respectfully toward better choices, our lives begin to end in a slow and destructive pattern. We become a part of the problem, not the solution.

When we seek to legitimize choices that oppose life or destigmatize barrier-behaviors so as to appease the faction of the population that wishes to make destructive choices without consequences, we must consider the direction in which this trend would lead humanity. When accommodating ideals that seek to change what is good in favor of what is popular, we risk compromising the world of the future rather than improving it. If we strive to excuse bad choices, do we not deter personal responsibility? The way to advance human potential is to raise the bar, not set it on the ground.

The Natural Choices – Gardening experts recommend that bulb plants be allowed to die off naturally in order to promote growth the following season.

> "One of the visual problems with spring bulbs is the foliage that remains after bloom. The foliage can become unsightly if the bulbs are planted in a public area of the landscape. Foliage should not be mowed off until it turns yellow and dies back naturally" (http://urbanext.illinois.edu).

When a bulb plant is in the dying process, it may not seem attractive, and we may not be at ease with its natural progression, but the life-choice is to let it happen as nature intended, so that new life may spring from its source in the coming season. If we mow down the foliage or pull off the dead leaves, we damage the plant's ability to renew itself. Nature has a developed a way of extending its life. Interfering with natural processes is often counter-productive to life-giving stages. We are challenged to take the natural course, and make the decisions that cause the least amount of harm to life.

Natural family planning – The very basic science of natural family planning offers women more self-reliance and control in dealing with their reproductive systems than any unnatural means. Natural family planning is the *green* alternative to harmful chemicals that often have powerful side-effects. By studying and understanding the essential components of women's reproductive system, any woman can make the life-giving choices that give her the means to work with her own natural rhythms. It is truly amazing how many people have a superior understanding of an iphone, for instance, and all the functions, apps, and possibilities, and with great ease they can operate it to satisfy their ultimate goals. Yet, understanding the nature of our own bodies - how they work, what they need to be healthy, how we can protect them from harm - is a skill best left to others?

Women have the power to understand their own fertility, their cycles, and their capabilities without the constraints of chemicals, gadgets and devices that can not only interfere with the natural process of lovemaking but also leave a woman ignorant of the natural beauty of her own body, and cause harmful side effects. Artificial contraceptives can be compared with any other non-organic approach to nature, just as organic approaches are considered an environmentally friendly and natural approach to planning a family because they foster healthy processes without the use of chemicals, genetically modified organisms, pesticides, hormones and nanomaterials. Is it considered sensible to purchase organic foods, environmentally friendly products, and exercise, but turn around and perform unnatural methods of birth control? It would seem these choices are inconsistent.

There are many times when female fertility issues, cycles and normal rhythms present a health concern. In such cases it is wise to consult with a medical doctor for assistance. Quite often, the medical issues encountered by men and women alike result from a deficiency in nutrients, an overindulgence in processed or fatty foods, or an irregular exercise regimen. A natural approach to addressing health issues should be an important consideration. Marilyn Shannon, nutritionist, biochemist, and author of *Fertility Cycles and Nutrition* recommends,

> "Nutrition and medical care are by no means mutually exclusive. A good medical doctor's ability to diagnose, treat, and advise is a blessing we are fortunate to have. In my opinion, however, once a diagnosis is made, healing through nutrition should ordinarily be considered the *first resort*. If intervention with drugs or surgery becomes necessary, the importance and value of excellent nutrition is even greater."

Many health concerns that women experience can be addressed through proper nutrition and natural measures. When pharmaceutical drugs become the first line of defense, it becomes a choice that inhibits a more life-affirming measure. If women are being made to feel like drugs are the best or only choice, they are prevented from exploring more life-friendly alternatives. Contraceptive drugs, chemicals, and devices are far from natural approaches and do not necessarily promote optimum health.

Artificial contraception leaves a woman with a false sense of control over her own body. In fact, she relinquishes control to pharmaceuticals. In many areas of modern life we have surrendered our authority over our own health to farmers who use unhealthy farming techniques to produce our food; we allow the medical industry to negotiate our well-being with drug companies, insurance companies, and quite possibly even a government health programs. In order to command more control over our own lives, we have forfeited the desire to choose life in order to make other choices.

Contraception – modern rhetoric is now addressing medical coverage of contraception, abortifacients, and abortions as a "Women's Health

Issue" which frightens women away from natural thinking, green living, and life-affirming choices. Pregnancy is not a disease or disorder – it is the natural result of the natural act of sexual intercourse. Pregnancy may be an unwanted condition but it is not a health hazard unless the woman is unhealthy or the fetus is unviable. In order to regain our natural understanding of human sexuality, we must rediscover its beauty and without focusing so heavily on how to stop life!

In a letter to Melinda Gates (of the Bill and Melinda Gates Foundation), a Nigerian woman and biomedical scientist, Obianuju Ekeocha, responded to a proposed gift to infuse Africa with 4.6 billion dollar worth of contraceptive drugs and devices by saying,

> "Even at a glance, anyone could see that the unlimited and easy availability of contraceptives in Africa would surely increase infidelity and sexual promiscuity as sex is presented by this multi-billion dollar project as a casual pleasure sport that can indeed come with no strings - or babies - attached. Think of the exponential spread of HIV and other STDs as men and women with abundant access to contraceptives take up multiple, concurrent sex partners. And of course there are bound to be inconsistencies and failures in the use of these drugs and devices, so health complications could result; one of which is unintended abortion. Add also other health risks such as cancer, blood clots, etc... The moment these huge amounts of contraceptive drugs and devices are injected into the roots of our society, they will undoubtedly start to erode and poison the moral sexual ethics that have been woven into our societal DNA by our faith..." (http://www.teresatomeo.com).

Ms. Ekeocha suggests that instead of donating 4.6 billion dollars for contraceptives in Africa, the funding would be more helpful in areas that are needed –

> "We need: Good healthcare systems (especially prenatal, neonatal and pediatric care), food programs for young children, good higher education opportunities, chastity programs, support for micro-business opportunities for women, fortify already established NGOs that are aimed at protecting women from sex-trafficking, prostitution, forced marriage, child labor, domestic violence, sex crimes, etc... $4.6 billion dollars can indeed be your legacy to Africa and other poor parts of the world. But let it be a legacy that leads life, love and laughter into the world in need" (http://www.teresatomeo.com).

The message is clear: non-profit organizations, philanthropists, charities, and social justice efforts can be aimed at choosing life-alternatives – programs that support life, rather than contra-life programs that work against it. Quality of life can be enhanced by programs aimed at sustaining healthy living, not by reducing life opportunities. The same principles of life-choices can be encouraged at both the level of individual decisions as well as corporate and humanitarian efforts. We love humanity by helping life along, not by curtailing it; and we love ourselves by ascending to a higher standard.

We are challenged, therefore, to love our bodies with the intent of doing no harm; we are confronted with an opportunity to respect ourselves as a fully functioning human being with the power to give life and to reject immoral practices; we are faced with the many chances to love at a supreme level that extends beyond ourselves; and our desire for harmony is continually tested. How will we respond? By attesting to the integrity, dignity and value of life – our own, and that of others - we can be confident that our choices will safeguard each and every precious human being on the planet.

When as an individual, a community, a nation, or a human race, we endeavor to place a *choose life* goal at the forefront of our decisions, we can avoid the dangerous pitfalls of choices that are, in essence, anti-life. Dr. Alan Guttmacher of IPPF when speaking about population control, emphatically stated that,

> "Each country will have to decide its own form of coercion and determine when and how it should be employed. At present, the means available are compulsory sterilization and compulsory abortion. Perhaps someday a way of enforcing compulsory birth control will be feasible."

Statements such as these are not only contra-life, but also contra-choice. Such rhetoric has also raised alarm signals among minority communities. Pastor Glenard Childress, Jr. of Blackgenocide.org is outraged, not by an overtly compulsory birth control agenda, but by the resolute influence of Planned Parenthood over the past few decades to convince minorities that contraception is for "economic betterment and health measure." He writes, "Alan Guttmacher, then president of Planned Parenthood, was desperate to show policy-makers that birth control would produce a situation whereby 'minority groups who constantly outbreed the majority will no longer persist in doing so. . .'"

In the words of the late Nellie Gray, "If everybody doesn't have a right to life, then nobody has a right to life." Each and every one of our choices matter; and in each decision there is the opportunity to *choose life* – not only to benefit ourselves but to benefit everyone. Our choices should be embedded with a sense of respect for life, and this often means that we must rise up to defend it.

Abortion

"Whoever destroys the life of a single human being, it is as if he destroyed an entire world and whoever preserves the life of a single human being, it is as if he preserved the life of an entire world" (The Mishnah, Sanhedrin 4:5).

Abortion is not an isolated concept limited to the act of terminating a pregnancy – by confining this noun to an abstract without considering *the action* and *the result* is to minimize its total impact. Natural pregnancy is a condition resulting from the natural act of sexual intercourse between a man and a woman. The result of this condition, if allowed to continue to its natural end, is the birth of a child. Abortion, however, is the action that results in the termination of a life - permanently. What is terminated is not just a condition of pregnancy, but a human life as well. In the past few decades, more attention and fervor has been awarded to the choice to terminate. In modern times, it would seem that defending a woman's choice to terminate overrides defending a woman's choice to sustain a pregnancy and to give life, and the result is that woman's choice to abort a fetus takes precedence over the child's right to life. Life and Choice – two interconnected forces, are in direct conflict with one another. We must seriously consider the bigger picture. In making a choice to abort a fetus, one is making a permanent commitment to a choice that negates the possibility of changing one's mind later on, and making a different choice – it is a severely limiting and irrevocable choice. When we choose life, we opt for choices that are not destructive, neither in the short-term, nor in the long-term; we leave possibilities open for changing our minds and making new choices. We cannot know the outcome of our choices in advance, but by choosing life we support our own free will to choose again.

Women deserve better choices than terminating someone's life as a solution to a problem. An unwanted pregnancy is not equitable with compulsory child-bearing – it's about making a loving choice. As a society, we can learn to be more inclusive of all that it means to make life-choices. When we exclude choices that allow us to amend a decision, we have severely limited the entire concept of "choice." We can help women to make life-choices by supporting them through difficulties. Choosing life should not be the choice that is frowned-upon. For over three decades, our culture has been inundated with jargon that assuages a woman's right to choose abortion. Essentially, it is a decision not to choose life. Just as significant is the fact that once the choice is made to abort, it's a decision that cannot be undone; she cannot change her mind once it is completed. Each abortion destroys countless future choices – it is technically, therefore, not "pro-choice." Only *life* guarantees limitless opportunities to make choices.

True acceptance adheres to the inclusion of people with disabilities, and there has been an ongoing effort to support people with special needs in education, business and industry, and the social environment.

While the continuing endeavor strives to raise awareness of disabilities and works to build inclusive and caring communities, there is an opposite endeavor to ban inclusion of people with disabilities by denying them a right to life. While prenatal tests can identify many disabilities, there is no prenatal test to determine whether a child with disabilities, or one without disabilities, will have an enriched and successful life. In order to be truly inclusive and accepting of people with disabilities, we choose life no matter what the circumstances. As a parent writing for the National Dissemination Center for Children with Disabilities, Patricia McGill-Smith shared the following,

> "This person is your child, first and foremost. Your child's development may be different from that of other children, but this does not make your child less valuable, less human, less important, or in less need of your love and parenting. Love and enjoy your child. The child comes first; the disability comes second. If you can relax and take the positive steps just outlined, one at a time, you will do the best you can, your child will benefit, and you can look forward to the future with hope" (http://nichcy.org/).

Choosing life is a supreme act of love. Parents of children with disabilities have discovered an unprecedented ability to love by respecting the dignity of all human life. Aborting a child, any child, eliminates the possibility of loving that child. There is no *organic* foundation for the practice of abortion as its only purpose is to end the possibility of one's existence. It is not a green alternative for the betterment of humanity. One doesn't eliminate a perfectly good crop, or a perfectly good species, or a human being perfectly capable of love. Should not saving a human fetus rank somewhere above saving a whale or dolphin, a rainforest or watershed? Abortion is not a loving choice and it should never be a preferred choice over choosing life. In 1983, President Ronald Reagan in Abortion and the Conscience of a Nation said that

> "Every legislator, every doctor, and every citizen needs to recognize that the real issue is whether to affirm and protect the sanctity of all human life, or to embrace a social ethic where some human lives are valued and others are not."

On a college campus one day, a professor of sociology geared his topic of morning water cooler conversation toward the current issues facing the state legislature by elucidating on the problem of priorities. He maintained that lawmakers should not have to continually revisit the abortion and contraception issue all the time; that the established policies are valid with regard to women's rights, so that they should focus their energies on other, more important issues. The young woman with whom he was speaking nodded her head in agreement and began to list issues that were more important: jobs, the price of gas, etc... Later that day a grave news report hit the campus that another school shooting had killed three students at Chardon High School in Northeastern Ohio. The young woman, who had been considering certain issues to be more important than abortion and contraception, declared in a loud voice, "You see, our representatives should be focusing on stopping kids from killing each other." What the professor of sociology and the young woman failed to see is the inconsistency of their convictions. Kids are getting mixed messages – where it's acceptable to take a life in one venue, it is unacceptable in another. Until our impressionable children begin to receive a consistent message to respect *all life*, and that all forms of ending human life are wrong, it will be very difficult to reform these societal issues.

Euthanasia

"Euthanasia means any action committed or omitted for the purpose of causing or hastening the death of a human being after birth, allegedly for the purpose of ending the person's suffering" (Brian Clowes, Ph. D., *The Facts of Life*). Clowes argues that the conflict over death with dignity "arises over the definition of dignity." He goes on to explain that,

> "Pro-euthanasia activists perceive a loss of physical or intellectual dignity when a person becomes incontinent, incoherent and confused, suffers intractable pain, or feels that he has lost control of his destiny. Anti-euthanasia activists perceive a loss of spiritual dignity when a person loses his focus on God and instead desire only a release from an existence that he or others may find pointless and wasteful.... However, when a person can overcome his fear of both death and pain, and accept and transcend them with a deep peace at the end of his life, he realizes that purely physical measure of 'dignity' are inappropriate. True compassion demands that all of us love and support one another regardless of our functional capacity or appearance, and prepare the dying for their ultimate meeting with God. This is the true definition of living with dignity, even when dying."

As with contraception and abortion, euthanasia has the indelible mark of being a non-organic practice – it has no life-affirming purpose. As being green has the connotation of protecting life from destructive influences, euthanasia is a system of endangering the value of human life. When the worth of a human life is measured by the prospect of longevity, the degree of pain, or one's usefulness, we inhibit the distinctive clarity of vision that serves to evaluate our full human potential: our ability to make the best of each moment regardless of how many moments remain, the capacity to rise above pain and suffering so that life has greater value than its physical properties, and the power to acknowledge that the gift of usefulness may be something that is unseen at the moment.

Alternatively, when a person enters a hospice program the goals focus on the complete palliative care and well-being of the patient rather than expediting the dying process. Care of the terminally ill in hospice does not include extraordinary measures to prolong or shorten the life of the patient; treatment ensures that the whole human being is nurtured physically, emotionally, and spiritually. This care is extended to family members as well, who may be dealing with the trauma of losing a loved one. Hospice is a life-choice that respects the natural dignity of the dying process. Every effort is made to honor the wishes of the person at the end of life with the understanding that death is a normal part of life. Euthanasia, on the other hand, is the act of assisting a person to die. It enables the process of death and is therefore not a life-affirming choice.

Life is filled with choices. Life is the only thing there is that provides us with choices, even if at times it seems that our choices are few – without life there are no choices at all! We must develop an inner attitude to choose life in all things. When circumstances arise that make life-giving choices difficult, it is important to seek counsel – however, if you seek the counsel of someone who has no stake in your issue, how can you trust them to help you make a life-affirming choice? Those in the position of counseling who focus on getting rid of a problem rather than solving it may not be offering the kind of life-giving choice that will help you; they may be causing further harm.

The value of a human life is not calculated by a monetary figure. Its true value lies in the capacity of one human life *to love,* and we are all challenged to love to the highest level that we possibly can. Each human being, from the moment of conception until natural death deserves the chance to love to this level; when we make a choice that denies a person this chance to love we are robbing the world of an immeasurable resource. Making life choices provides the world with this resource; we are giving rather than depleting the world of the most valuable resource we have. Taking a life-for-a-life is not an equitable solution to the problems of crime as seen in punishments that include the death penalty. The possibility of atonement and reform is extinguished. Transformation, atonement, and the choice to relearn love have been restricted. Extinguishing life is equivalent to extinguishing possibilities.

By putting all of the life-issues on the same page, we can reach an understanding of how some solutions afford each of us with an opportunity to love unconditionally and without limits, and how other solutions actually perpetuate a problem by eliminating a choice to love. When we love and choose life, the benefits are countless, but when violent solutions to society's problems are a means to avoid them rather than working through them to find peaceful solutions, we perpetuate violence. Restricting life is an aggressive act that is prone to subjectivity. It sends the message that violence is tolerated with appropriate reasoning. The prevalent crises of abuse, crime, school shootings, euthanasia, and abortion are all violent solutions to personal problems that someone is facing each day. Just as diplomacy is advocated as a peaceful resolution to predicaments, searching for counseling as an alternative to abuse is a peaceful solution. Abortion is a violent solution to the problem of an unwanted pregnancy. Helping women to find options other than abortion is a diplomatic way to preserve a life, and the dignity of a woman. She does not have to feel like it's her right to commit this violence because society enables her. Focusing on life-values, initiating peacekeeping measures (such as SAVE) into schools to counteract bullying, are non-violent solutions to the problems of students who see violence as their only option.

When the choices are most difficult is precisely when the most care should be taken to make decisions. Choosing options that terminate life is something that we often find difficult to live with. We are creatures that strive for life – we try to extend it, to enhance it, to manipulate it, and to benefit it, but terminating it causes a wounding cognitive dissonance when our actions put an end to life. This discord, again, can only be assuaged by 1) not terminating life, or 2) seeking justification to do so.

Life thoughts

Life and choice are inherently intertwined. We would not wish to live life without choices, and we find it difficult to live with choices that end life. In order to harmonize our dissonance we can practice living a life that supports life choices. It's time to heal our brokenness by recognizing the choices that hurt, destroy, cause others to suffer, and take away a special opportunity to love. Though extraordinary choices may come with complications, they should be seen as a chance to love more deeply than we ever dreamed possible.

The Circle of Choice

Tammy Worth, writing for the *Health* section of the LA Times investigated the problem of modern culture inundated with an onslaught of choices. In her article: "Too Many Choices Can Tax the Brain, Research Shows" Worth explores the inconveniences and burdens of having too many choices to contend with on a daily basis. She writes that,

> "...when people have too many decisions to make -- consumers end up making poor decisions, are more dissatisfied with their choices or become paralyzed and don't choose at all. It also leads people to make poorer choices -- sometimes at a time when the choice really matters..." (LA Times).

With so many choices that overwhelm us on any given day, is it any wonder that making a simple decision about cereal brands and bottled water varieties can have an anesthetizing effect on the more critical decisions that impact our relationships, our lifestyles, and our ability to learn from past decisions? As individuals and as a human race we need to reclaim our ability to make life-affirming, greener choices without marketing gurus, fraudulent schemers, a biased media, misguided entertainers, and cunning politicians telling us what is right for us. Life, well-lived, well-shared, well-cared-for, and well-chosen has more widespread benefits than trying to satisfy fleeting trends. We need to reexamine the motivations behind our choices. Do our decisions seem to be need-driven, or want-driven? Are we easily swayed by what everyone else is doing or are we employing unselfing habits in order to make room for decisions that benefit others?

Each person has at least a general idea of the things that they care about and regularly tries to make decisions with the value of the issues in mind. Frequently, there are choices within choices that we must consider; these layers of choices can complicate our decisions even though we have the best of intentions. We know that we should make healthier food choices, but cost becomes a factor; we're aware that we need to eradicate unhealthy habits such as smoking, but our dependency compromises our decision to quit; we'd like to make better decisions in our relationships, but fear of being alone or disliked may affect the course we choose. We are always confronted with internal factors that influence the ultimate decision. We can choose to cut our high-tech gadgets cost in order to purchase organic food. We can choose to heal our issues and dependencies so as to eliminate our unhealthy habits. We can choose to overcome our fears and insecurities to strengthen and improve our relationships. Getting to the root of our choices requires a bit more effort initially; yet, integrating all our internal choices aimed at a life-affirming objective will eventually translate into optimal living.

When we consider the larger choices, the issues that we sometimes focus on rather than our personal habits, we can see how they are all related to the bigger scheme of things. We desire peace-not war; we wish to end poverty and substandard living; we are against animal cruelty; we are in opposition to domestic violence and child abuse; we seek to cure AIDS, Diabetes, Cancer, etc…; we want quality of life for the elderly and disabled; we want a healthier environment with cleaner air and water; we aspire to quality education for our children; we want to save endangered species and the rain forests; we wish to eradicate crime- drug use, thefts, murder, rape, pedophilia; we want to put an end to genocide and human trafficking and slavery; we want to end the choices that destroy human life; we desire prison reform to keep society safe – all of these issues that are vital to human life have one thing in common – choosing life means we care about *all* of the above, not just some of them. Only by consolidating all of these issues and recognizing the direct link between our personal decision-making and the state of the world in which we live can we begin to make the choices that will transform our lives. Only when we cease to create divisions between people of good will and strive for better unity can we begin to affect the changes to the issues we know to be critically important to the quality of human life. We need to raise awareness about choosing life and exactly what that means. It doesn't mean one thing with respect to one issue and something else when considering another. Choosing life means putting all important values on the same page and working together to heal and grow and generate a spirit of revitalization on a global scale so that every form of life on this planet benefits from the respect and protection it deserves. Defending life doesn't mean defending some life and not others – it means defending *all* life. In order to be a truly *green*, we must live up to a responsibility of caring for each facet of life and stop marginalizing some portion of it in order to rationalize our desires. Consistency brings results!

Raising self-awareness, by identifying barrier behaviors, and reducing their influence on our decisions helps us to enhance the wellspring of resources that augment a joy-filled life. We should learn to recognize the impediments to making loving decisions. Obstacles to life-affirming choices can include random decision-making that neglect thoughtful outcomes, and in-vogue choices. Random choices make it impossible to stay on a steady course. When we are indolent about the importance of our choices, we jump on the current bandwagon, or become swept away by a tide of bad cultural choices so that we are in danger of following a non-life-giving path, laden with confusing pitfalls that do not lead to peace. If all of humanity were to simultaneously follow the trendy path that may not choose life along the way, we would soon find that, although we are all together, we are not headed for peace, but in unison, we may be heading toward ever-increasing conflict. The road to peace is a simultaneously individual road and a unified road, a one-person vehicle traveling on a crowded highway. While an individual making a choice for himself alone doesn't appear to affect anyone else, the fact is that no one on the crowded highway is truly alone. If a person were to make a bad personal choice, it has a ripple effect. If millions of people make the same bad choice, the effects are astronomical. The more important our decisions, the more love and responsibility are required to make them. Extraordinary choices are weighty; they are often the most difficult ones to make and they require the most love to make them.

Historical author and lecturer, Gene Pisale wrote, "Every sunrise is a new chance- to right something that was wrong, to correct yesterday's mistakes, to do what was left undone and a fresh start on a new and better path, the right one, in your life..."

We make mistakes. Being fully human does not mean that we are perfect or that we don't often fail to make the best choices. Being *fully human* means that we are continually in the process of getting better all the time. We do this by recognizing when we have made a mistake, by having remorse for our shortcomings, and by making amends to the best of our abilities so that we avoid the mistake in the future. In order to become better, to love better, to foster life in a better way, we must be vigilant in recognizing those times when we fail to do so. Atonement is progress while denial dumps us in the opposite direction. We can only break the cycle of injustice by rectifying wounding habits and building life-giving strategies that have both personal and large-scale results. Forgiveness has the power to heal – it follows the recognition of injustice, but demands that we don't remain stagnant in that recognition. We identify the wrong, but we mustn't remain grounded in finger-pointing. Getting stuck in the critical faction does not allow for growth. Instead, we need to find ways to become part of the healing process and to move forward by discovering opportunities to grow beyond the problems and working for solutions. Avoiding barrier behaviors that impede progress means redirecting our actions and using the tools of life. If problems persist in friendships and families, neighborhoods and communities, public, private, and even religious institutions, we can be a part of the healing endeavor by finding solutions and discovering the key choices that heal. If we all make loving choices, the ripple effect will bring about *true* change and viable progress, but we must be consistent.

It is time to spread the message of life; it is time to restore goodness by backing up our values with life-oriented objectives; and it is time to recognize the damage that barrier-behaviors can inflict when we listen to the messages that try to confuse us. These inconsistent messages distract us from a set course directed at life and love, and shift the focus back on to selfish behaviors or compartmentalized thinking that blind us and prevent us from seeing the bigger picture. When we stand up for true justice which includes *all life*, and speak up for all who have no voice; when we work to build life-affirming relationships and communities, we will see the change we *all* wish to see, regardless of race, creed, gender, or age.

Our hope in a new kind of world that respects life and what it means to be human - so that we can *all* live life to the fullest - should motivate each of us to do our part to advance life-choices. Diminishing the value of life undermines the importance of survival. When we support the natural world and the spirit of love that lives within each of us by avoiding finite choices, we grow cooperatively, not alone. As long as we support our own conflicting goals, when what I want as an individual contradicts itself by choosing life sometimes and not others, our goals will not exist in harmony with our actions and peace will continue to elude us. Sometimes we make choices that we believe will solve a problem and make us happier but if it's not a life choice, happiness remains out-of-reach. In order to have a truly full life we must make choices that support and give rein to the fullness of life. Whenever we do, life grows. We must learn to subject our selfness to lifeness so that the indomitable human spirit can reach its greatest heights.

Imagine if we all worked together to build a life-giving world, plant goodness, enjoy the fruits of life, expand and multiply beauty, increase the value of humanity, promote the well-being of all, heal our relationships with each other and with God, listen to the undercurrents of life, work toward a consistent idea of hope which includes everyone, look for opportunities to heal our divisions, transform external healing into an internal remedy, show love and compassion, soften the world with gentleness, and take the steps that lead to a higher form of happiness. A global transformation which endeavors to put life first would be a change worth embracing! As interconnected as we are by the ribbons of DNA, we are also profoundly related by a desire for peace and goodwill, but consistency in achieving this goal is paramount.

We each have a lifetime to get this right, to use each and every precious day of our lives to make loving choices. Our choices and decisions shape our lives. The strength of love empowers us. It restores, it soothes, it heals and it triumphs. Love and life are co-supporting. Together they have the power to put an end to destructive tendencies and make room for productive change. When we synchronize our acceptance of the wonderment of life, we recognize that each person is truly wonderful and deserving of the best choices that life has to offer. We must be unified, for without a consistent effort to honor life, there can be no peace. We recognize that we can all participate in protecting one another from choices that destroy life. We all want the same things, though we may be coming at it from different angles, we all want the best that life has to offer. When we begin with a life-choice we continue into more life choices. It is time to stop choosing sides and start choosing life. We need to come together and form habits that direct our decisions in a life-giving direction. If we wish to live in a better world, we begin by choosing life in each decision we make, no matter how small or how large: Choose Life.

Life thoughts in their own words,

Black Elk Oglala Sioux Holy Man, 1863-1950

> "You have noticed that everything as Indian does is in a circle, and that is because the Power of the World always works in circles, and everything tries to be round..... The Sky is round, and I have heard that the earth is round like a ball, and so are all the stars. The wind, in its greatest power, whirls. Birds make their nest in circles, for theirs is the same religion as ours....
>
> Even the seasons form a great circle in their changing, and always come back again to where they were. The life of a man

is a circle from childhood to childhood, and so it is in everything where power moves."

Rev. Billy Graham,

"We have lost our spiritual equilibrium and reversed our values. We have exploited the poor and called it the lottery. We have rewarded laziness and called it welfare. We have killed our unborn and called it choice. We have shot abortionists and called it justifiable. We have neglected to discipline our children and called it building self esteem. We have abused power and called it politics. We have coveted our neighbor's possessions and called it ambition. We have polluted the air with profanity and pornography and called it freedom of expression. We have ridiculed the time-honored values of our forefathers and called it enlightenment."

Pope Benedict XVI,

"Openness to life is at the centre of true development. When a society moves towards the denial or suppression of life, it ends up no longer finding the necessary motivation and energy to strive for man's true good. If personal and social sensitivity towards the acceptance of a new life is lost, then other forms of acceptance that are valuable for society also wither away. The acceptance of life strengthens moral fiber and makes people capable of mutual help. By cultivating openness to life, wealthy peoples can better understand the needs of poor ones, they can avoid employing huge economic and intellectual resources to satisfy the selfish desires of their own citizens, and instead, they can promote virtuous action within the perspective of production that is morally sound and marked by solidarity, respecting the fundamental right to life of every people and every individual."

Eagle Chief (Letakos-Lesa) Pawnee

"In the beginning of all things, wisdom and knowledge were with the animals, for Tirawa, the One Above, did not speak directly to man. He sent certain animals to tell men that he showed himself through the beast, and that from them, and from the stars and the sun and moon should man learn.. all things tell of Tirawa. All things in the world are two. In our minds we are two, good and evil. With our eyes we see two things, things that are fair and things that are ugly.... We have the right hand that strikes and makes for evil, and we have the left hand full of kindness, near the heart. One foot may lead us to an evil way, the other foot may lead us to a good. So are all things two, all two."

Quatsinas (Hereditary Chief Edward Moody) Nuxalk Nation:

"We must protect the forests for our children, grandchildren and children yet to be born. We must protect the forests for those who can't speak for themselves such as the birds, animals, fish and trees."

Thomas Merton:

"Our job is to love others without stopping to inquire whether or not they are worthy. That is not our business and, in fact, it is nobody's business. What we are asked to do is to love, and this love itself will render both ourselves and our neighbors worthy."

Chief Dan George:

"When Christ said that man does not live by bread alone, he spoke of a hunger. This hunger was not the hunger of the body. It was not the hunger for bread. He spoke of a hunger that begins deep down in the very depths of our being. He spoke of a need as vital as breath. He spoke of our hunger for love. Love is something you and I must have. We must have it because our spirit feeds upon it. We must have it because without it we become weak and faint. Without love our self-esteem weakens. Without it our courage fails. Without love we can no longer look out confidently at the world… But with love, we are creative. With it, we march tirelessly. With it, and with it alone, we are able to sacrifice for others."

Hubert Humphrey:

"It was once said that the moral test of government is how that government treats those who are in the dawn of life, the children; those who are in the twilight of life, the elderly; and those who are in the shadows of life, the sick, the needy and the handicapped."

Abraham Lincoln:

"And in the end, it's not the years in your life that count, but the life in your years."

Deuteronomy Ch. 30:19:

"I call heaven and earth to witness against you today, that I have set before you life and death, blessing and curse. Therefore choose life, that you and your offspring may live."

Mother Teresa of Calcutta:

"Life is an opportunity, benefit from it.

Life is beauty, admire it.
Life is bliss, taste it.

Life is a dream, realize it.
Life is a challenge, meet it.
Life is a duty, complete it.
Life is a game, play it.
Life is a promise, fulfill it.
Life is sorrow, overcome it.
Life is a song, sing it.
Life is a struggle, accept it.
Life is a tragedy, confront it.
Life is an adventure, dare it.
Life is luck, make it.
Life is too precious, do not destroy it.
Life is life, fight for it."

Author's Note

There are many dangers associated with compartmentalizing our choices. We may choose life in one compartment, and make a harmful choice in another and we're unhappy with the results. Religious affiliations aside, the option to choose life, to make that choice which benefits the entire species, would seem in all cases to be the best alternative. Of course we have the right to choose, we have always had this right. The consistent choice for a better world is to give life a chance – choose life in everything we say and everything we do. If we work to apply a central, governing method or routine to all the choices we make we can come to realize the potential of our innate humanity. It's never easy. It requires a consistent application and a determined effort to put impulses and old habits aside.

This book is the result of a challenge, a confrontation that forced me to analyze, not only what I claimed to stand for, but the reasons for my point of view. Such was the case when I purchased my Choose Life license plates from the Virginia Department of Motor Vehicles several years ago. What I soon discovered as I drove my little car around town and to work was that this license plate was associated with a greater responsibility than I originally imagined. For one thing, I had to drive in a manner which lived up to my message. Also, mine was the only car on a traditionally liberal campus to sport this kind of *propaganda,* and as such I had to scrutinize my words and behavior more carefully.

One day, after parking my vehicle in the faculty lot, I was routinely making my way toward my first class when a young woman coming from the student lot caught up with me. As a former student, she first greeted me earnestly, then immediately commented on the cuteness of my small vehicle but once she observed my Choose Life plate she fashioned a second judgment, "So, you're against abortion, huh?"

I glanced at my plate and back at my student, recognizing this as one of those accountability moments and I realized that some of the changes I'd made in my life had been directly affected by a decision to consolidate my choices - the routine behaviors integrated with the a conscious resolution. When I responded with the idea that I was trying to put all my choices on the same page, my student didn't quite understand my answer. I replied to her with a short explanation but this book comprises the lengthier version and is a compilation of the thought processes that attempt to put life choices into deliberated routines. To make each decision based on a life-giving design is a calculated effort to be more fully human. Choose Life routines are an ongoing process to implement a life-giving motto into every conceivable decision in life. This reflection has caused me to take a much closer look at what it means to be "pro-life." It is important to consider the bigger picture when determining "a procedure established in advance of an eventuality" which affects long-term as well as short-term consequences. A careful examination of life choices requires an open-mindedness that accepts responsibility for the self as well as a conscious concern for the benefit of humanity. I am grateful to God for the promptings I received along the way while writing this book and for the love and patience of my family, friends, husband and children who always provide my life with a very special meaning and purpose.

D.K.

About the Author

Donna Kendall, author of the fiction novel *Sailing on an Ocean of Tears*, memoir *Dancing with Bianchina*, and children's books *Stitch-A-Story* and *Uncle Charlie's Soup*, also writes for the DC Examiner, and has published a number of short stories and poems in literary journals. She teaches writing courses at Northern Virginia Community College, works in hospice, and volunteers as a librarian. She lives with her husband in Northern Virginia.

Bibliography

Aristotle. *Nicomachean Ethics.* Trans. J.A.K. Thomson. London: Penguin Books, 1953.

Barker, Phil. "Cognitive Dissonance." *Beyond Intractability, University of Colorado, Boulder.* http://www.beyondintractability.org September, 2003.

Bok, Sissela. *Lying: Moral Choice in Public and Private Life.* Vintage Books, 1999.

Brasted, Toni. "Benefits of Prayer." http://compassioncarehospice.com

Brennan, Joe. "Aging with Dignity." http://www.agingpositively.com

Briggs, George, M. and Doris Howes Calloway. *Nutrition and Physical Fitness.* Philadelphia: W.B. Saunders Company, 1979.

Burnett, Francis Hodgson. *The Secret Garden.* Pavilion Press, 2004.

Callahan, Sidney. "Lured by the Spirit to an Ethical Life." National Catholic Reporter. http://natcath.org/http://natcath.org/ December, 2002.

Child Welfare Information Gateway. "How Parental Substance Use Disorders Affect Children." *U.S. Department of Health and Human Services: Administration for Children and Families.* http://www.childwelfare.gov

Childress, Rev. Clenard H. Jr. http://blackgenocide.org/home.html 2012.

Clowes, Brian. *The Facts of Life: An Authoritative Guide to Life and Family Issues.* Front Royal: Human Life International, 2000.

DeMauro, Laurie. *Ethics: Opposing Viewpoints.* Greenhaven, 2006.

Dickens, Charles. *A Christmas Carol.* New York: Bantam Classics, 2009.

Dillon, Robin S. Ed. *Dignity, Character, and Self-Respect.* New York: Routledge, 1995.

Dillon, Robin S. "Respect." *Stanford University Encyclopedia of Philosophy.* http://plato.stanford.edu/entries/respect/ Fall, 2010.

Eberstadt, Mary. *Adam and Eve After the Pill: Paradoxes of the Sexual Revolution.* San Francisco: Ignatius Press, 2012.

Eberstadt, Mary. "Eminem is Right." *Policy Review, No. 128.* Hoover Institution Stanford University, http://www.hoover.org., 2004.

Ekeocha, Obianuju. "A Letter to Melinda Gates." http://www.teresatomeo.com/342-a-letter-to-melinda-gates-the-contraception-controversy-342.html August, 2012.

Emerson, Ralph Waldo. *The Conduct of Life.* Ed. H.G. Callaway. New York: Rowman and Littlefield, 2006.

Ericson, Edward. *The Humanist Way: An Intro to Ethical Humanist Religion.* New York: Continuum, 1988.

Ethics Resource Center. "The Importance of Ethical Culture: Increasing Trust and Driving Down Risks." Arlington: Ethics Resource Center, 2010.

Family and Child. http://www.homemorals.com/moral-value/honesty/index.html

Foster, Gregory, D. "Ethics: Time to Revisit the Basics." *Thehumanist.org.* The American Humanist Association, March/April, 2003.

Goleman, Daniel. *Emotional Intelligence: Why It Can Matter More Than IQ.* New York: Bantam Books, 1995.

Grohol, John. "How Indifference Can Kill a Relationship." *World of Psychology.* http://psychcentral.com/

Hamblen, Jean Dana. "Turning Tragedy into Triumph." http://www.sooperarticles.com/self-improvement December, 2009.

Hay, Louise L. "Keep Your Thoughts Healthy: Know Your Inner Messengers." You Can Heal Your Life. http://www.healyourlife.com/author-louise-l-hay/2009/10/lifeshelp/get-healthy/keep-your-thoughts-healthy October, 2009.

Heschel, Abraham Joshua. *Who is Man?* Palo Alto: Stanford University Press, 1965.

Hoffer, Eric. *The Ordeal of Change.* Cutchogue: Buccaneer Books, 1976.

Hymowitz, Kay S. *Ready or Not: Why Treating Our Children as Small Adults Endangers Their Future and Ours.* San Francisco: Encounter Books, 2000.

Hymowitz, Kay S. "Tweens: Ten Going on Sixteen." *City Journal,* Autumn, 1998.

http://www.asktheinternettherapist.com/

www.auscharity.org at http://makeadiff.wordpress.com/

http://mathoverflow.net/

http://onelife.com/index.html

http://urbanext.illinois.edu/bulbs/planting.cfm

http://www.au.af.mil

http://www.cleanairgardening.com/

http://www.cnn.com/interactive/2012/03/world/mauritania.slaverys.last.stronghold/index.html

http://www.drugabuse.gov/

http://www.hinduism.co

http://www.holisticmedicine.org/

http://www.introducingislam.org

http://www.medterms.com

https://www.osha.gov/

http://www.vachoose-life.org/

http://www.wisegeek.com/

Hugo, Victor. *Les Misérables*. Trans. Charles E. Wilbour. New York: Fawcett Books, 1961.

Ilibagiza, Immaculée with Steve Erwin. *Left to Tell. Discovering God Amidst the Rwandan Holocaust*. Carlsbad: Hay House, 2006.

Jackson, Jill. "Let There Be Peace On Earth." http://www.humanmedia.org

Johnson, Steve. http://www.scu.edu/ethics/about/people/directors/school/johnson/

Krishnan, Mini. "Building a Safer World." India Education Review, Concept and Series Editor, Oxford University Press.

Lewis, C. S. *Mere Christianity.* San Francisco: Harper, 1952.

Lewis, C. S. *The Abolition of Man.* New York: Collier Books, 1962.

Mansour, Rabbi Eli J. "Trickery, Lying, and Deceiving, Are Forms of Stealing: Geneivat Da'at – Thievery Through Deception." *The Rabbi Jacob S. Kassin Memorial Halachic Series,* http://www.dailyhalacha.com, Aug. 2012.

Maslow, Abraham. "A Theory of Human Motivation." *Psychological Review, Vol. 50 #4,* 1943.

Marquis, Don. "Archygrams." *Archy a Life of Mehitabel.* http://www.donmarquis.org/.

Mayo Clinic Staff. "The Arithmetic of Forgiveness." http://www.mayoclinic.com/health-information.

McConnell, John. "77 Theses on the Care of the Earth." http://www.earthsite.org/77.htm

McLeod, Carolyn. "Trust." *Stanford Encyclopedia of Philosophy.* http://plato.stanford.edu/entries/trust/ Feb. 2006.

Mork, Rachel. "Gratitude and Other Stress Relievers." Life 123. http://www.life123.com/health/stress-management. 2012.

The Holy Bible, New International Version. Grand Rapids: Zondervan, 1990.

O'Brien, Michael D. *A Landscape with Dragons: The Battle for Your Child's Mind.* San Francisco: Ignatius Press, 1998.

Post, Emily. "Best Society." http://www.bartleby.com

Pychyl, Timothy A. "A Hierarchy of Excuses: The Pathetic Path of Least Resistance." *Psychology Today*. http://www.psychologytoday.com, March, 2011.

Reagan, Ronald. *Abortion and the Conscience of a Nation*. Sacramento: New Regency Publishing, 2000.

Sasso, Rabbi Sandy Eisenberg. "Children's Spirituality." http://www.spiritualityandpractice.com

Schweitzer, Albert. *Civilization and Ethics*. Unwin Books, 1961.

Shannon, Marilyn M. *Fertility Cycles and Nutrition*. Cincinnati: The Couple to Couple League International, Inc., 2001.

Scott, Sherrie. "Examples of Integrity in the Workplace." http://smallbusiness.chron.com/examples-integrity-workplace-10906.html. 2012.

Singer, Peter, and Jim Mason. *The Ethics of Food Choices: Why Our Food Choices Matter*. Rodale: Holtzbrink Publishers, 2006.

Smedes, Lewis, B. *My God and I: A Spiritual Memoir*. Cambridge: Wm. B. Eerdmans Publishing Co., 2003.

Smith, Patricia McGill. "You Are Not Alone." *National Dissemination Center for Children with Disabilities*. (http://nichcy.org/families-community/notalone October, 2010.

Students Against Violence Everywhere. http://nationalsave.org/main/history.php 2012.

Talbot, John Michael. *Blessings, Reflections on the Beatitudes*. New York: The Crossroad Publishing Company, 1991.

The Society for Cultural Anthropology. "Life and Death, A Conversation." http: //sca.culanth.org/about.htm

Thomas, Rosario. *The Philosophy of Life: The Pope and the Right to Life.* Pro Fabritus Press, 1989.

Worth, Tammy. "Too many Choices Can Tax the Brain Research Shows." *LA Times.* http://articles.latimes.com/2009/mar/16/health/he-choices16 March, 2009.

Z., Michael. "Humility is Not Thinking Less About Yourself, But Thinking About Yourself Less." http://www.selfgrowth.com/articles/

Zaragoza, Federico Mayor. "The Ethics of the Future." UNESCO, April, 1998.